Profiles in Emergent Biliteracy

Educational
PSYCHOLOGY

Critical Pedagogical Perspectives

Greg S. Goodman, *General Editor*

Vol. 9

The Educational Psychology series is part of the Peter Lang Education list.
Every volume is peer reviewed and meets
the highest quality standards for content and production.

PETER LANG
New York • Washington, D.C./Baltimore • Bern
Frankfurt • Berlin • Brussels • Vienna • Oxford

M. CATHRENE CONNERY

Profiles in Emergent Biliteracy

Children Making Meaning in a Chicano Community

PETER LANG
New York • Washington, D.C./Baltimore • Bern
Frankfurt • Berlin • Brussels • Vienna • Oxford

Library of Congress Cataloging-in-Publication Data

Connery, M. Cathrene.
Portraits in emergent biliteracy: children making meaning in a Chicano community /
M. Cathrene Connery.
p. cm. — (Educational psychology: critical pedagogical perspectives; v. 9)
Includes bibliographical references and index.
1. Mexican American children—Education (Elementary)—Case studies.
2. Bilingual education—United States—Case studies. 3. Mexican Americans—
Social conditions—Case studies. I. Title.
LC2683.3.C66   372.1829'6872073—dc23   2011029460
ISBN 978-1-4331-0863-1 (hardcover)
ISBN 978-1-4331-0862-4 (paperback)
ISSN 1943-8109

Bibliographic information published by **Die Deutsche Nationalbibliothek**.
Die Deutsche Nationalbibliothek lists this publication in the "Deutsche
Nationalbibliografie"; detailed bibliographic data is available
on the Internet at http://dnb.d-nb.de/.

The paper in this book meets the guidelines for permanence and durability
of the Committee on Production Guidelines for Book Longevity
of the Council of Library Resources.

© 2011 Peter Lang Publishing, Inc., New York
29 Broadway, 18th floor, New York, NY 10006
www.peterlang.com

Printed in the United States of America

To V. who gracefully and graciously, gratefully
journeyed
beside me
this
very long
way.

Contents

Acknowledgments

The succesful creation of any book is a collective experience. I am deeply grateful to the many children, friends and colleagues whose assistance, expertise, or kindness positively contributed to this manuscript. My profound appreciation is, first and foremost, extended to the anonymous *hijitos*, families, and fellow educators who participated in my doctoral dissertation. I wish to thank my dissertation committee members, Drs. Vera John Steiner, Holbrook Mahn, Edward DeSantis, and Ernie Stringer; administrators who opened key doors, including Ms. Dora Ortiz, David Rodgers, and Dr. Leroy Ortiz; outstanding teachers and friends Chip Winn Wells, Paula Campbell, Jessica Karstetter, Laurie DeHaven, Nicole Walker, James Durham, Karen Higgins, Avie McCoy, Dr. Christina Curran; my first chair extraordinaire David Shorr; and distant mentor/role model Dr. Patricia Richard Amato, who knows how to pick a great Italian restaurant.

In addition, the following collaborators read and commented on the manuscript, including Dr. David Freeman, Dr. Josie Tinajero, Dr. Eugene Garcia, Dr. Sue Menig, Carol Mowry, Trina Lannegan, and Nancy Schnebly; my patient and wise editor and coach, Greg Goodman; Sophie Appel and the production crew at Peter Lang; and the extraordinary Bonita Ferguson.

I appreciate Ithaca College's Education Department for funding the assistance of two outstanding graduate assistants: Rebecca James and Patti Levine. Much thanks to these teacher education candidates (soon available for hire!) for providing such a high quality of support and insight despite a grueling schedule. Finally, my serenity and gratitude goes to H.P., the V.G, Mary L., Janet, Big Bri (told you so) and the Sunday Morning Crew: you sustain me.

CHAPTER ONE

Welcome to the Gallegos Barrio

The Guadalupe Bridge arches over rusted rail yards before dropping gracefully into the barrio. At the foot of the decline, most drivers turn their leased vehicles sharply to the right, being careful not to hit the junkies frequenting the intersection. But when the street is clear and the light turns green at the exact right moment, it is possible to ride the sweet flow of gravity straight into *el corazón de la comunidad*–the heart of the community. *Bienvenidos*. Welcome to Gallegos, a proud American neighborhood, nestled within our patriotic, 47th state of New Mexico.

La Ciudad: The City

Just north of the *barrio*, a small cluster of skyscrapers, banks, and government buildings stands politely to the side of a great chocolate river. Ambulances regularly scream past legal, judicial, and law enforcement workers enjoying lunch at trendy cafes. Sunshine and knicknacks attract tourists into southwestern-themed pawn shops and quaint stores with dollars from afar. At a closer glance, it appears that with the exception of a giant convention center, the city's fiscal health is sadly dependent on the misfortune of its residents. Riches amassed from poor health, miseducation, and criminal activity provide a steady economic base for the municipal government. After five p.m., heavy wrought iron bars make it difficult to discriminate between businesses closed for the evening and those storefronts abandoned years ago. Neon bar lights attract a steady stream of customers in the supply–demand of a night–day economy recycled in downtown courtrooms.

El Barrio Gallegos: The Gallegos Neighborhood

The bus route divides the neighborhood of Gallegos from the inner city. With the exception of a few strategically placed sculptures and tiled bus stop benches, much-lauded revitalization efforts side-stepped the *barrio*. A bitter irony haunts this municipal neglect: the historic Gallegos once attracted fame and fortune to the city, hosting movie stars and other wealthy railroad passengers during the 1930s. Today, its residents vacuum the red carpeted floors of an up-scale, surround-sound theatre just up the street. Yet, in a state known for commercializing colonization into quaintness, *los Galleños*–the people of Gallegos–know that girder by cement slab, pot by dish, trash bin by bath towel, the city belongs to them.

La gente–the people–have come to endure the dust and roar of incessant traffic associated with urban sprawl. As the city expanded, Gallegos became isolated amidst a tangled web of concrete ribbons leading away from the southern shadow of the concrete epicenter. With the exception of a long-standing salsa factory and a Mexican *mercado* selling convenience products at dramatically inflated rates, *las familias* must travel outside the neighborhood to purchase their daily bread. The city's modern and well-kept Science Park provides the only impetus for non-neighborhood residents and visitors to journey down Gallegos' cottonwood and elm-lined streets.

Tiny, grey-fenced yards give way to gravel gardens and dirt-packed driveways crowded with broken cars. Ramshackle garages lean into dingy cottages housing recent immigrants as a secondary means of mortgage payment. Poverty and economic blight are evidenced by yellow, substandard housing notices posted on doors, the stink of raw sewage, and multiple layers of trash caught in fences flying down streets. Piles of shattered glass lie undisturbed in the street for several weeks. Alcoholics bump cracks in the sidewalk with stolen shopping carts loaded with their worldly possessions.

For the most part, Gallegos is quiet during the day. Women wait for men to return from work before venturing outside their homes. Residents of the neighborhood complain the local news media paints a distorted image of Gallegos; newspaper editors refer to the barrio as a part of the city's "war zone." Occasionally, horizontal police cars block neighborhood side streets hastily parked by cops dressed in full battalion commando. Emergency calls lead the officers to alleys and burned-out buildings where an addict has overdosed or a prostitute has been severely beaten. Long lines of steel track provide an easy escape route behind a well-established string of crack houses.

In daylight, the presence of *las pandillas,* or gangs, is limited to the discovery of freshly scrawled graffiti. A few *pachuchos* (gang members) cruise the blocks of Gallegos in shiny low riders. At night, a counter-economy surfaces to conduct business and defend turf. Highly organized, local, regional, and national gangs compete in a financial game of cat and mouse without rules. Occasionally, gun shots and heartbreak shatter the innocence of childhood; violence blurs real life when underground business goes bad. *Los vecinos* or neighbors still talk about a young family who watched television with their windows open to escape the city's summer heat. Breezy drapes hid the shadows of drug dealers seeking revenge. After incorrectly identifying the family's apartment, their hit man wedged a gun between the window bars of a wrought iron screen only to unload an entire case. A pre-schooler was killed in the mistaken shooting.

Cultural Institutions of Gallegos

However, first impressions of the neighborhood are misleading. While many of the city's inhabitants associate Gallegos with the grit of street violence, the violence of gang warfare does not appropriately represent the character or life of the *barrio*. In the hazy, yellow-gray sunshine, the true neighborhood is like an ambiguous item wrapped tightly in cheesecloth. Unwinding the package reveals the strength, courage, and color of *la gente*–the people–as they advance in their five hundred year-old struggle to thrive. Statues of *La Virgin* quietly guard shadowed sills with drapes once used as sheets. Between makeshift apartments and injured furniture, cracked adobe homes sport giant, gleaming Ford Broncos with loads of lumber extending from their beds. Many of the men of Gallegos climb into their trucks at four-thirty a.m. to work fifteen-hour shifts, six days a week. Plastic flowers bloom on the porches of retirees who dutifully rise to sweep their steps each morning. The determination of the Galleños to live and love family and friends forges a keen sense of ingenuity, humor, and connection strong enough to stand tragedy and time.

The residents of Gallegos display a rich sense of cultural pride. In keeping with its Mexican-American heritage, vibrant murals relate the neighborhood's history and iconography. At the local neighborhood center, middle school students practice Aztec dances, pounding bare feet to drum beat on a dusty gym floor. In the late afternoons, *mariachi* band members can be seen stealing a smoke in church driveways before wedding ceremonies begin. Their brocaded, ornamental suits are artfully sewn by expert seamstresses, accented with individually handcrafted silver buttons. The opening of a local Latino Arts Museum across the highway showcased the literary, visual, culinary, and performance art forms perfected by *los Galleños* for centuries. In its archives, relatives pore over vast genealogical records to identify their *antepasados*–ancestors who passed before them–who first settled the area during the 1500s. At the museum's yearly chile festival, *primos* ride on top of their cousins' shoulders, munching on corncobs. A traditional dance troupe from Juarez performs for the local elementary school. The children cheer their age mates as their compatriots deftly swarm the stage, twisting and flashing brightly colored skirts like sunflowers in a high wind. The value placed on family, culture, and youth is reflected in the living curriculum of Mariposa Elementary, Gallegos' neighborhood school.

La Familia: Extended Family as Cultural Context

There is a wealth in Gallegos unseen in the upscale neighborhoods north of the city. Families of fifteen barbecue on driveways using giant propane skillets to ensure everyone is fed. Babies are kissed, hugged, and passed among male and female relatives alike, each assigning their own pet name to the child. After completing a circle of arms, dangling keys, and googling eyes, their *tíos*– aunts and uncles—cradle the baby until she sleeps.

In Gallegos, grandfathers walk their *nietos* to school, tightly holding their grandchildren's hands for the full six or seven blocks. If a forgotten lunch is discovered, grandmothers will rewrap fresh, warm tortillas or an occasional *biscochito* in foil for the inattentive child. Their spouses are warned not to break the sugar cookie at the bottom of the greasy paper sack when delivering the missing lunch. For the first three years of school, many primary students cannot name the cafeteria food, preferring red *chile*, rice, and potato burritos from home. In Gallegos, the Latino tradition of caring for youth—placing children at the forefront of the family—is observable in a multitude of everyday routines and life ways. While parents might struggle to provide the same material means and security assurances wealthier families do, *los hijos de Gallegos son muy queridos*. The sons and daughters of Gallegos are well loved.

Meet Nuestros Hijos, or the Boys

The heart of the *barrio* is located at the corner of Garcia and Perrea Streets. There, two little boys attempt to build a makeshift bike ramp from items they have scavenged from their families' possessions. Toño awkwardly wields a borrowed hammer heavier than his arm while Beto patiently, but warily, slides and steadies a fresh plank into place. As we venture closer, we notice the children use two languages to shout at each other above the clumsy bang of iron against wood and the occasional ring of a nail. Let's walk up so I can introduce you to the children.

Les Presento Umberto "Beto" Joel Chavez y Mendoza

Beto is a happy, mellow six-year-old with brown eyes and shiny black hair. His small, round face eases into shy, warm smiles after seriously, yet imperceptibly, surveying his environment. Beto's deliberate and easy movements are confidently executed from well-considered cues. When the kind child is not helping a family member in some task, Beto enjoys riding bikes or playing at the park with his older siblings. As the youngest of four children, Beto delights in wrestling with his strong 'apa. A list of Beto's favorites includes plain hamburgers, fiestas con su familia, animals, and the color blue. He has an affinity for babies, turtles, interesting machines, and funny television shows. His buzz haircut is accented by a thin, ten-inch braid, stemming at the base of his neck. The wavy strands, grown since birth, poke through a hole in his gora. Beto is a sweet, wise hijito in a blue-and-white mesh tank top with shorts to match.

Meet Antonio "Toño" Miguel Ortiz-Anaya

Antonio or "Toño" is a cheerful, spry six-year-old with lively, green eyes and light brown hair. His small, elfish-like face is quick to smile and expressively react to the constant flow of color and conversation around him. Toño's petite frame remains in constant motion, exploring, manipulating, and interacting with his environment. When he is not watching cartoons or playing video games, Toño enjoys building imaginary landscapes and action figures from the natural objects and trash he finds around his home. As the youngest of three children, Toño's impish grin reveals great delight when he has succeeded in getting his twelve-year-old sister in trouble with his parents. A list of Toño's favorites includes pizza, holidays, animals, and the color green. He is mesmerized by life underwater, dinosaurs, geodes, how birds can fly, and the amount of spice that can stick to his fingers when eating Cheetos. Toño is a creative, inquisitive force of energy captured in tiny brown sandals, a camouflage T-shirt, and basketball shorts two sizes too big for him.

Multilingual Biliterates: An Untapped National Resource

While the presence of multilingual and biliterate children like Beto and Toño dates back to the earliest epochs of American educational history (Crawford, 2004; Kloss, 1977), districts have recently witnessed a dramatic increase in the number of linguistically diverse or language-rich students in our nation's schools. Between 1989 and 2000, the total number of elementary and secondary heritage, bilingual, and English language learners (ELLs) rose approximately one hundred and four percent (U.S. Census, 2000). In 1979, 3.8 million school-aged children spoke a primary language other than English. By 2008, this statistic jumped to 10.9 million students. In the 2007–2008 academic year alone, bilingual children constituted 21% of all five-to-seventeen year-olds enrolled in K–12 classrooms (NCES, 2010). Demographics suggest that, by the year 2020, a quarter of all U.S. school children will speak a language other than English at dinner.

Traditionally, linguistically rich children who enter school speaking a non–English language are incorrectly viewed as academically and socially deficient. Educators refer to this deficit by identifying students with the acronyms LEP (limited English proficient), PHLOTE (primary home language other than English), and ESL (English as a second language). More recently, an emphasis has been placed on the abilities of linguistically rich students as ELLs (English language learners) or EAL (English as an Additional Language). However, this designation fails to capture the cultural or linguistic assets children like Beto and Toño acquire, develop, and utilize as culturally diverse, multilingual, and biliterate students.

History points to the fact that, tragically, we have failed to view our children's linguistic and cultural traditions as an American resource. Deficit ideologies have fostered destructive myths about the value of multilingualism. These false notions have prompted the majority of educational districts to adopt policies and practices that seek to eliminate children's home languages and replace them with English, often at great expense. At the same time global institutions, including the World Bank and International Monetary Fund, emphasize an urgent need for a multilingual and biliterate citizenry. Within the United States, this call has largely been absent from the national conversation regarding school reform.

Both domestic events and international trends demand our reconsideration of educational practices that ineffectively replace one form of monolingualism with another. Indeed, the realization of our nation's promise is dependent upon our ability to recognize the biliterate potential of *all* K–12 children as an untapped source of national strength, security, and pride.

About This Book

Purpose of the Text

Toward this end, this book explores the emergent biliteracy development of Toño and Beto as they were learning to speak, listen, read and write in academic Spanish and English at the same time. The work presents the kindergarteners' progress in my dual-immersion classroom for half an academic year, into the long days of summer when we continued to explore their worlds through oral and written language. The text portrays the boys' emergent and evolving proficiencies across a critical nine-month period.

Biliteracy is the holistic, interdependent practice of listening, speaking, reading, and writing proficiencies from two linguistic and cultural systems to make meaning (Goodman, Goodman, and Flores, 1979; de la Luz-Reyes, 2001; Perez and Torres-Guzman, 1996). In focusing on the initial phase of this process, we witness the children's early attempts to transact their personal life experience while becoming apprenticed into the larger historical-political, sociocultural communities that surround them (Echiburu-Berzins & Lopez, 2001). By observing the creation of Beto and Toño's aural, oral, pictorial, and written texts in Spanish and English, we are able to appreciate the complexity of emergent biliteracy as a creative process with both common and unique features.

We are also privy to view the beneficial, additive, and generative social construction of the children's language and literacy foundations or linguistic reservoirs, confirming what Moll (2001) describes as the "primary advantage of biliteracy...the intellectual breadth it can facilitate, the expended possibilities found in developing new social and literate relationships to mediate children's academic learning" (p. 20).

Motivation for the Study

The motivations prompting the larger study from which this book was derived are rooted in personal and professional experiences. Growing up, I experienced profound forms of academic marginalization throughout most of my schooling. These memories compelled me to provide my students with the best education I could offer, first as an art instructor and later as a content-ESL and dual-immersion elementary classroom teacher. In preparing lessons, I sought not to just teach, but to reach the children for whom I sat en parentis loci.

As an Irish-American, English-dominant female, my life and initial educational experiences did not appropriately prepare me to meet the needs of my culturally and linguistically diverse students. I was shocked by the overt racism exhibited by many of my colleagues and coworkers toward children like Beto and Toño and their families. While I have been privileged to be a part of the larger effort to nurture joyful, proficient, and successful biliterates, I have also witnessed the needless suffering, self-doubt, loss of potential, and low esteem of too many linguistically rich children across the course of my career. Therefore, the overriding purpose of this book is to improve teacher candidates', educators', researchers', and policy makers' understanding of emergent biliteracy and the linguistically diverse children we are privileged to serve.

About the Investigation

The larger investigation was based on the writings of a Russian scholar, Lev Semenovich Vygotsky, and contemporary scholars of sociocultural or cultural-historical theory (see John-Steiner, 1999; 1995; 1992; 1991; Mahn, 1997; Mahn and John-Steiner, 2002; John-Steiner and Mahn, 1996; John-Steiner, Meehan and Mahn, 1998; John-Steiner, Panofsky, and Smith, 1994; Wells and Claxton, 2002; Lee and Smagorinsky, 2000; Moll, 1990; Cole, 1996; 1990, etc.). This theoretical-analytical framework explains complex psychological experiences like learning and biliteracy as the "dynamic interdependence of social and individual processes" by examining the themes of "development, co-construction, synthesis, knowledge transformation, and semiotic mediation" (John-Steiner, 1999, p. 2). Vygotsky offers us a rich, conceptual lens through which we can view and understand Toño and Beto's biliteracy development.

A Qualitative, Microgenetic Action Research Study

In order to best capture and relate the children's growth, I adopted a qualitative research method which allows researchers to conduct studies within authentic, real-life contexts (Bruner, 1983). I additionally applied a microgenetic research design to appropriately investigate the developmental nature of Beto and Toño's meaning making. Vygotsky himself used this approach to capture, analyze and explain the dynamics of psychological processes as they occur "in flight" (Vygotsky, 1978, p. 68). Microgenetic researchers collect multiple, in–depth, observations that allow them to "return to the source and reconstruct all the points in the development of a given structure" (Vygotsky, 1978, p. 65). In this manner, we can understand the transformations, successive approximations, and profound changes that occur in the development of psychological processes (Siegler and Crowley, 1991; Wertsch, 1985; Panofsky, 1999).

The investigation additionally drew on features of action research outlined by Stringer (1999; 2004). This form of scientific inquiry merges theory and practice to highlight and enhance the lived experiences of its participants during and after the research process. Denzin and Lincoln (2000) portray action researchers as social scientists "committed to a set of disciplined, material practices that produce radical, democratizing transformations in the civic sphere" (p. 32). By observing, reflecting, and re–presenting the lived experience of Toño, Beto, and their families, the study sought to discover and relate "the real, material, concrete, particular practices of a particular people in particular places with an eye toward changing particular practitioners' particular practices" (Kemmis & McTaggart, 2000, p. 595) to enlighten entrepreneurial, health care, academic, and political entities (LeCompte & Preissle, 1993). In keeping with the descriptive nature of this research stance, factual, scientific protocols resulted in the creation of the case accounts presented in the chapters to highlight the lived experience of young participants.

The Research Methodology

I first began the nine-month study by asking how linguistically rich kindergarteners make meaning when acquiring the processes of listening, speaking, reading, and writing in two languages. I was interested in what their thinking was like both inside and outside dual-language classrooms and school settings. A series of sub-questions emerged from the main question during the research process. These inquiries included: What is literacy? What does the initial acquisition of biliterate proficiencies look like? How do linguistically rich children construct meaning? Under what circumstances does emergent biliteracy develop and how can it be facilitated inside and outside the school context?

In order to answer these questions, I collected a variety of data from a multitude of empirical materials. Data were systematically gathered for six months while the children attended my half-day kindergarten. During the summer months, data was also produced and collected during experiential sessions in which the boys participated in outings to local museums and parks. These excursions were followed by representational sessions whereby we met at the local library, where we discussed and captured Beto and Toño's impressions, understandings, and meanings of our visits.

By the end of the study, a diverse collection of resources had been amassed. Multi-modal information was derived from field notes, formal observations, photographs, video and audiotape transcriptions, artwork, writing, and dictated stories created by myself and the children. Parental permission provided access to Toño and Beto's schoolwork and institutional documents. Data from these materials were used to analyze, triangulate, and construct a brief sociocultural history of each family, a general instructional outline of our time spent together, emergent biliteracy chronologies for each child, as well as multi-modal accounts of Beto and Toño's individual experiences of a common outing to the local biopark, among other items. In keeping with qualitative research methodologies, these texts were then unified to present highly detailed, factual portraits of the emergent biliteracy and meaning-making processes of our two young friends.

Focus of Each Chapter

This first chapter has set the scene for Toño and Beto's case accounts. The description of the children's city, neighborhood, and cultural institutions locates the Gallegos Barrio as a larger site and source for their emergent biliteracy development. In chapter two, we enter the Chavez and Ortiz–Anaya homes to meet the boys' families and obtain a glimpse of their history, including the funds of knowledge, and language and literary practices that help to shape Beto and Toño's growth as emergent biliterates. We discover a little about the neighborhood elementary school in chapter three, including the circumstances surrounding each boy's induction into the formal educational system. Chapter four provides a window into our bilingual kindergarten, including a curricular and instructional backdrop of a typical day. Toño and Beto's ontogenesis or development as emergent biliterates during the academic year is related in chapter five. We then accompany the children to a Science Park, obtain an in-depth view of the boys' portraits of meaning making in chapter six. Chapter seven highlights how Beto and Toño transacted elements of this experience using their newly acquired dual-language proficiencies in Spanish and English. In the eighth chapter, we draw understandings about this distinct semiotic process from the boys' nine-month developmental trajectories. Finally, chapter nine concludes the text with a list of guidelines for educators interested in nurturing emergent biliteracy on behalf of young children.

Languages of Presentation

Naturalistic inquiry and action research methods seek to preserve and reflect the authentic voices and experiences of individual participants engaged in the study. Therefore, in order to honor Beto, Toño, and the boys' families' literacy practices, both Spanish and English texts are incorporated into this book. Specific sections of text are presented in Spanish to highlight authentic language use. These segments are translated in italics when their direct meaning is required for the English-dominant reader. In other instances, Spanish translations do not occur, as a means of authentically retaining and relating the integrity of the childrens' lived experience. In these cases, the surrounding text has been crafted to scaffold meaning for the non-Spanish literate. English-dominant readers may potentially transact with these sections in a manner similar to meaning makers acquiring a second or additional language. On a few occasions, both English and Spanish texts are successively noted, indicating the common practice of code switching employed by the boys, their families, and members of the larger Gallegos community

A Word for Educators

This book was born of the desire to connect with and honor the linguistically rich child, grounded on the belief that the alleged "language barrier" many educators erect between themselves and their students is no more than a false, cultural edifice—an imaginary, ideological barricade—constructed from ignorance and fear. Recognition and remediation of my own inadequacies as a person and a professional allow me the privilege of continuing to learn that the best educator is one who is able to remain open to experiencing the world through the eyes, heart and mind of children. Regardless of our own personal circumstances, educational development, or life experiences, it is our professional responsibility to expand our understanding of the linguistically rich children and biliterate potentials we are responsible for and privileged to serve.

Now that we've met up with the boys, let's begin to tear down this wall by passing through the doorways of the place they call home. We'll venture back in time to Toño and Beto's birthdays. All relatives, friends, and visitors that enter are welcomed warmly. Stepping across the thresholds of ethnicity, class, and language, we are invited into the warmth of kitchens and embraced by the mingling scent of hot, sweet tortillas, a strong hug and *besitos* on the cheek.

CHAPTER TWO

In the Arms of Family

By the time Juana and her *suegra* put the last of the dinner dishes away, her husband snored loudly on the living room couch. Juana breathed heavily into another contraction as her mother-in-law shushed the children to avoid waking their father. She had ridden waves of pain like this before. As the pregnant woman lumbered into the back bedroom, she hoped her baby would arrive soon enough for Eduardo to be present. The family could not afford for her husband to take a day off from work to witness the birth of his fourth child. Her first three children delivered quickly and— *Gracias a Dios*–the hardworking father had the chance to hold his son and two daughters moments after their births.

Within a few short hours, Juana's prayer was answered. Eduardo cradled a six-pound crying boy, or *llorón*, before leaving the hospital at sunrise. Across the course of the day, Umberto Joel Mendoza y Chavez's extended family were not to be prevented from holding him either. Relatives tiptoed past the nurse's station, ignoring the maximum occupancy signs in Spanish. When the other patient in Juana's room called for assistance, a nurse discovered five children and three adults sharing two wooden chairs at the side of her bed. Chiding them gently, the nurse herded all but two members of the extended family into the waiting room.

As the child's godfather, the infant's *padrino* remained close to mother and child until Eduardo's fourteen-hour shift was over. The steady stream of relatives marveled at the baby's head of thick, black hair and tender nature. While *el chapito* had been named for his spiritual guardian, Joel, the name "Umberto" also proved well chosen. By the time the family left the hospital, even the nurses agreed the baby's personality revealed a "bright heart." The nickname "Beto" immediately became a term of endearment for the contented infant. Beto's shortened name allowed his three siblings and many little cousins a simplified means of identifying their new baby. *El apodo* also served as a wellspring for subsequent nicknames. Rhyming with the Spanish word for tuna, "Betún" became his godfather's favorite childhood nickname for the little boy.

La Familia Chavez

As an American citizen, Beto's birth marked the success of a bi-national family, five generations in the making. Faced with starvation as a ravage of civil war, his *antepasados paternos* or ancestors were forced to leave their homeland of Mexico in search of work. Beto's *bisabuelo* returned to his great, great grandmother by whatever transportation he could arrange three to four times a year, carrying much needed food, supplies, and American dollars. The sons and grandsons of the dedicated patriarch followed in his responsible footsteps, providing the muscle that kept the American economy afloat during World War II. Like many other *braceros* or laborers, the Chavez men were never remunerated for deductions subtracted from their paychecks by both the Mexican and American governments.

As the eldest son of eight brothers, Beto's father was apprenticed into the construction business through connections his father and grandfather before him had established on both sides of the border. A moderately religious family, Eduardo *y sus hermanos* took great pride in sharing the same humble profession as Saint Joseph, the father of Jesus. Every Easter, the Chavez carpenters, framers, and builders make a pilgrimage with their families to a local chapel. Their ten-mile walk commemorates the sufferings of Christ while giving thanks for the blessings bestowed on the entire family for the year. Aunts, uncles, cousins, and friends of all ages *andan los cerros secos* with baby strollers, cameras, and water bottles as they have walked the dry hills to the shrine for several generations. After giving thanks at the sacred site, the entire family convenes in the mountains for a day of feasting and laughter.

Chavez Family Funds of Knowledge:
Linguistic, Occupational, and Educational Resources

As the youngest son of Mexican nationals, Beto was born into a family that placed a high priority on bilingualism. His family's survival and success in the United States requires literate proficiencies in at least two languages. Family sentiment embraced the popular *dicho,* or truth, that a single bilingual holds the worth of two people. The traditional structure of the Chavez family ranked according to financial contribution, birth order, and gender, as well as the bilingual proficiencies a member might contribute to the group as a whole. Neither Spanish nor English monolingualism was esteemed for the younger generation. Across the larger extended family, children were expected to respect and retain the language of their heart while acquiring the language of their new home and second country.

Economic demands prevented Beto's grandfather, father, and oldest brother from receiving formal schooling beyond the elementary years. However, the Chavez family clearly employed both informal and formal registers or styles of speaking the Spanish language. For example, their dialect was enhanced by linguistic structures and vocabulary from the Catholic masses they attended. This model of academic Spanish was complemented by discourse from a Cuban television channel that served as background to family conversations for most of the day. Eduardo's command of English included a few basic grammatical structures, conversational bits, and words essential to the construction industry. While his productive proficiencies in English remained limited, Beto's father developed a wide receptive ability in his second language as the result of business dealings on behalf of his father and brothers.

Beto's siblings exhibited bilingual proficiencies based on the amount of schooling each received since Eduardo and Juana had permanently immigrated to the United States nine years earlier. Eduardo Jr., a soft-spoken and gentle youth, loomed physically above his father. The oldest boy's lanky height and broad shoulders disguised him from compulsory school attendance laws enforced at most work sites. On occasion, Junior sympathized with less fluent Spanish-speaking visitors in the house by tossing one-word English lifesavers into a conversation. At first, Beto's mother, father, and oldest brother relied on their eldest daughter, Miranda, to translate interactions into English for them. Miranda proudly completed two years at Gallegos High School as the first female in her family to obtain any secondary education. Her marriage to a gifted mechanic from Chihuahua brought additional expertise and linguistic patterns into the family. While Rico spoke Spanish as his dominant language, his biliterate proficiencies included the ability to identify any car part ever produced in Spanish or English. Miranda's dream to obtain her GED would be realized after her two children were old enough to walk to Mariposa Elementary's Family Program. A highly intelligent woman, Miranda demonstrated a shrewd business sense and interest in the Internet.

The Chavez family's permanent move to the United States for the birth of their third child, Terecita, proved a wise decision. Juana's expert care of her youngest daughter was supported by her mother-in-law's adoration for the little girl. The two women hummed to the child, played patty-cake, chatted during household chores, and marveled at their favorite *telenovela* stars in Spanish. After school, Miranda played "teacher" with her little sister, reading books from her English as a Second Language class at school. By the time Terecita enrolled in Mariposa Elementary's dual immersion kindergarten where the child would learn to speak, listen, read, and write in Spanish and English, the family eagerly awaited Beto's arrival.

In time, Miranda's role as eldest sister naturally expanded into the family's first ambassador of academic English: playing school eventually transitioned into homework and read-aloud sessions. Out of respect for their mother, the children's use of English remained limited to academic tasks. As Terecita progressed through elementary school, code-switching and English discourse became more frequent between the youngest siblings, although Spanish remained the children's preferred language of choice. Juana's songs, language games, and extended conversations with Tere built a strong linguistic foundation for the little girl's Spanish literacy. Because Mariposa Elementary's program extended the Chavez family's literacy in a systematic and developmental manner, by fifth grade, Terecita usurped Miranda's role as chief translator to become the family's most "balanced" bilingual, fluently moving back and forth between Spanish and English in most situations.

Biliteracy Practices: Gender, Numeracy, and Narrative

Conversations in Eduardo and Juana's home conformed closely to gender roles and birth order expectations. Family members respectfully spoke one at a time in calm, lowered voices; children politely waited for older individuals to complete their thoughts. Silence carried great significance in the Chavez family's discourse or conversational patterns. Because the men's work outside the home required an intimate knowledge of measurement, quantity, value, materials, and on-the-job politics, Junior and Rico listened carefully as Eduardo and Joel discussed money, work, and economic issues. Women's labor inside the home employed a sophisticated understanding of food preparation, child development, family politics, and human psychology. As a result, Terecita overheard Juana and Miranda's verbal exchanges with grandmothers and aunts regarding the care of and collaboration with extended family members.

The men's discourse of numeracy intersected with the women's narrative discourse in complementary activities: Once a week, Juana and Eduardo made a major shopping trip to a large discount store. At other junctures, these gender-based communicative patterns appeared to be distinct from each other. After a grueling workday, Eduardo and Junior ate dinner in silence at the family's two-seat table. The rest of the family respected their providers' need to replenish their energies after a long day of physical labor. The caring husband, father, and older brother were attentive to the rest of the family's stories after their meal and nap.

The juxtaposition of these gender-based discourses additionally divided literacy practices among family members. For example, gender roles dictated Eduardo and Junior's fluency in numbers including the calculation of complex geometric and algebraic problems on the construction site. On the other hand, Juana, Miranda, and Terecita engaged in specialized oral and written sign use regarding cooking, formal celebrations, group discipline, and human relationships. Extended family members offered cognitive, linguistic, and literary resources when elders needed to make an important decision. Cousins, friends, and neighbors were tapped as resources to fill out formal documents, speak to teachers and doctors, engage in library research, and other tasks.

Story reading was not traditionally practiced in the Chavez household. Because the world of books was not associated with the Chavez family's socioeconomic class in Mexico, for the most part, neither independent nor recreational reading were included in the family's daily routine. The domain of education, including homework, read alouds, and parent-teacher conferences, was assigned as women's work. This delegation was not based on any form of negative judgment, as the value of an education was highly esteemed in the Chavez family. However, school practices were associated with female literacy based on the division of everyday labor and availability to visit school during its hours of operation.

Biliteracy as a Treasured Aspiration and Asset

It would be a mistake to draw conclusions about the Chavez family's attitudes toward literacy based on the lack of printed materials observed in their home. A religious calendar proved to be the only written text in direct view within their two bedroom home. Pencils were difficult to locate when the need arose to jot down a phone number. Like many women of her generation, Beto's mother did not have the opportunity to attend school in rural Chihuahua. As the eldest girl, Juana had many chores and the roads were unsafe for females to walk alone. Her family could not afford the books, shoes, or loss of an extra pair of hands at home.

When her younger siblings were old enough to attend school, Juana first learned to read. While the other children played at recess, the tall girl slowly learned the Spanish syllables guided by a patient teacher. Unfortunately, the bell always seemed to ring before it was time to practice writing her letters. As a young adult, Juana memorized how to form the signs in the words she needed to write from time to time. Her writing abilities were limited to spelling her children's first names and her husband's surname. Her eldest daughter, Miranda, served as Juana's scribe, writing addresses, phone numbers, and other important information down for her mother.

However, Juana understood the power of literacy better than all of Beto's family members. She stored Terecita and Beto's *papeles* confirming the children's citizenship and social security numbers in special plastic folders and boxes. Juana astutely intercepted written correspondence from her children's school, asking family and friends to translate or explain the meaning of the academic documents. Her closet contained a collection of *recuerdos* in written form including her girls' certificates of graduation from kindergarten, titles to family cars, poetry written by a sister, her children's grade reports, Eduardo's first birthday greeting, and a mass card from her father's funeral. Like many mothers of Catholic families, Juana guarded the Chavez library of baptismal bibles by hiding them away for safekeeping. With such literate artifacts tucked out of sight, their protected status exalted biliteracy.

While limited financial resources prevented the purchase of books, magazines, cards, and other materials associated with middle-class literacy, Juana impressed the need for her children to learn to read and write in Spanish and English. Miranda, Terecita, and Beto were expected to succeed in school and behave in a manner that did not bring shame on the family. Toward this end, Juana walked her children to school on time each day. At the main doors, she placed her *queridos* in the hands of teachers she considered an extension of herself. In the Mexican tradition, Beto's mother attributed teachers with the larger responsibility of educating as opposed to merely instructing her children.

During lunch time, Juana reassumed her obligations as a nurturing mother. In the same ritual she performed with her husband and children at home, Juana stood at the head of Beto's lunch table in the school cafeteria to open milk cartons, encourage healthy food choices, and cut his lunch tray meals into more edible pieces. While she did not know specifically how to foster her children's biliteracy development, Juana deeply understood Miranda, Terecita, and Beto's futures depended on her respect for the written word. Despite her own limited schooling, Juana was *muy buena educada* and better versed about life than many individuals with advanced degrees.

Biliteracy, therefore, was valued as a tremendous asset in the Chavez household. Eduardo often referred to his father and brothers regarding written instructions, contracts, warranties, or other legal documents. Beto's grandfather paid a distant acquaintance for assistance in filling out his medical forms. Individuals outside the family circle were recruited for help in purchasing significant items like trucks, homes, and trailers. As Miranda and

Terecita grew into adolescence, the use of less desirable, third-party translators was reduced. Because the two girls did not always comprehend exactly what they were reading, Eduardo developed strong instincts and was quick to ask salespeople targeted questions through either of his daughters. In turn, both girls developed a shrewd business sense from their father.

While Miranda served as the family's first pioneer attending English as a Second Language classes at the secondary level, Terecita's enrollment in Mariposa Elementary's dual-immersion program produced the Chavez family's first generation, biliterate ambassador. Tere's course of study was designed to fully develop listening, speaking, reading, and writing proficiencies in both Spanish and English. The program also sought to enrich the children's content area knowledge in science, social studies, math, and health through multiple intelligences. In time, Terecita surpassed Miranda's English proficiencies, helping to more completely navigate Beto's induction into the academic culture. The shy, kind, and sometimes mischievous sister transported her youngest brother back and forth across a linguistic bridge between private and public, home and school, as well as Mexican and American cultures.

Linguistically Rich Children as Sociocultural Treasures

The linguistically rich students that enter our classrooms embody the success of a historical-political, intergenerational struggle to survive. As sons and daughters, they are sociocultural treasures that simultaneously represent their family's past, present, and future. Linguistically rich children reflect the human tapestry of our larger society. They include resident, immigrant, and indigenous Americans like the Chavez family. Our linguistically rich students speak a multitude of national, ethnic, tribal, and second languages including Spanish, Karen, and Diné and a variety of linguistic dialects including African American vernacular, and academic English. Similar to Beto and his siblings, these children personify a colorful array of ethnicities and socioeconomic classes, as well as religious, geographic, and cultural traditions. Like their English-speaking peers, linguistically rich students come from many walks of life. They arrive at school with diverse individual and familial funds of knowledge, personal histories, educational backgrounds, school expectations, and social experiences. The constellation of these factors collectively determines their unique academic and social needs.

While over 400 distinct languages can be heard in American classrooms, approximately 80% of all linguistically rich students are native Spanish speakers (Christian, 2006). As the largest ethnic minority in the United States,

Hispanic, Latino, and Chicano children represented 21% of the total number of K–12 students during the 2007–2008 academic year (NCES, 2010). During the same time period, approximately 2 million of 5-to-18 year olds spoke Spanish as their primary language (NCES, 2010). In 2008, the Pew Report noted that 70% of all Latino, Chicano, or Hispanic public school students spoke Spanish at home. It is interesting to note these heritage Spanish speakers were more likely to complete advanced foreign language classes in Russian, Japanese, French, and other languages when compared to their monolingual, English-speaking peers (NCES, 2003). Between 1993 and 2003, Hispanics accounted for 64% of all K–12 children added to public schools (Pew Foundation, 2006).

Demographics suggest by the year 2050, the number of Latino school-aged children will surpass their non-Hispanic, European-American peers (Pew Report, 2008). Many people mistakenly believe these Spanish–speaking children come from immigrant families who, fleeing economic or political persecution, have entered the United States illegally. This notion is incorrect. Statistics report that the average Latino, Chicano, or Hispanic student is a U.S. citizen. Many families, like the Ortiz–Anayas, established themselves in the region before the Mayflower arrived on eastern shores. Let's walk down the street and check in with the Ortiz–Anaya family to learn about their family history and how Toño represents their hopes and dreams.

The Ortiz-Anaya Family

Smoke from wood fires drifted lazily above the rooftops on the cold January morning that Toño was born. Because his parents' place of employment did not offer health insurance, Fred and Kathy whisked their son home from the hospital by four p.m. on the same afternoon. The squealing newborn was ushered into their modest home by his oldest brother, middle sister, and two excited maternal grandparents. As the workday drew to a close, the baby's godparents, aunts, uncles, cousins, neighbors, and family friends all met in the tiny rental house each had helped to arrange for the infant's welcome. After the three-room adobe became too crowded, the baby's *parientes* departed, promising to visit during the weekend.

Toño—as the tiny infant was nicknamed by his *abuelo*—represented the newest hope of a family who first settled the city over three hundred years ago. The baby's extended family held great aspirations for their newest member. Toño's *antepasados* had survived a long migration to the Southwest in the name of a Spanish king. His relatives helped to colonize the wilderness, only to watch their fate pass through the hands of three successive governments.

Under *los Americanos*, Toño's grandparents survived the overt racist oppression that persisted against Latinos through the early 1950s. His own parents, Kathy and Fred, came of age during the Civil Rights Movement. Each generation in the Anaya-Ortiz family suffered great hardships in their determination to thrive. The family's greatest pride was the purchase of Toño's grandparents' *adobe* in the center of the *barrio*. The baby's namesake appropriately captured the family's rise from abject poverty to working-class status. Like its etymological root, the child was expected to blossom or flower in a divine manner.

Familial Funds of Knowledge: Linguistic, Occupational, and Educational Resources

As the youngest son in a Chicano family, Toño is united with his Iberian, Mexican, and Mexican-American relatives through the Spanish language. Both Fred and Kathy attended school when children were beaten by educators for speaking their native tongue. In the forties and fifties, Toño's grandparents were instructed by Anglo educational authorities that speaking Spanish at home was harmful to their children. The youngest of seven children, Toño's mother remembers tears of frustration pouring down the proud face of her *'apa* at dinner. For a time, a forced silence fell over family meals as her respected elders struggled to speak haltingly in English. Eventually, Kathy's mother ceased talking altogether. This same practice was followed by generations of Latino parents who loved their children so much, they reluctantly relinquished the language of the cradle.

By the time Toño's grandpa abolished the English-only rule in his home, the effects of linguistic colonization had scarred the hierarchical relationships within the family. While Toño's *abuela* retained Spanish as her language of care, his grandpa spoke a pidgin, or less developed form, of English. At the age of six, his mother's teachers had convinced her the name Kathy was more socially acceptable than *Catalina*. Her Spanish proficiencies were reduced to a restricted number of verbal responses and a limited range of receptive abilities. To this day, Kathy grapples with the inability to relate significant moments of her life to an adoring mother who cannot always understand her daughter.

Trapped in a society that devalued the language, culture, and wisdom of her primary relationships, Kathy was pushed out the doors of an apathetic and often hostile school system before high school graduation. Fortunately, she began dating Fred soon afterward. Toño's parents formed a strong partnership, eliminating the financial need to participate in the counter-economy of Gallegos' gang culture. Their twenty-year commitment to each other, their children, and Kathy's aging parents remains a great source of pride. Regrettably, not all of Kathy and Fred's siblings were so lucky.

When big-name national hotel chains built among the skyscrapers two blocks from the Anaya's rental, Toño's parents waited five hours for an interview in a line that wrapped around a city block. The company's human resources department preferred hiring married couples with children from impoverished socioeconomic areas based on information from government educational databases and their own profit and productivity statistics. While Kathy was hired to work nights as a maid and laundry worker, Fred was assigned to the day shift. Toño's father was also required to work several hours of overtime on the weekends as the lead maintenance man whenever an emergency arose. This schedule eliminated any time for the couple to see each other, but there were mouths to be fed. Luckily, the manager at the hotel was good to the Anayas. When one of the children became sick, he sometimes granted Kathy or Fred a day off. The boss waived company policy because he did not want to replace his two most dependable, English-speaking workers.

Intense stress and exceptional demands placed on families raising children in a high-crime neighborhood weighed heavily on Kathy and Fred's minds. Rudy, Toño's oldest brother, moved out of the family's home after his first year of high school. When the Anayas were hired by the hotel chain, Kathy's mom retired after thirty-two years as a factory worker in order to care for Toño's older sister Marisol. During their earliest years, both Sol and Toño were cared for almost exclusively by their Spanish-speaking *abuela* and grandpa who spoke limited English with his *nietos*. The juggling of occupational and child care schedules resulted in an eclectic exposure to different registers of the Spanish and English languages.

The two youngest Anaya children were nurtured in a linguistic nest by native, second-language, and heritage-language speakers of both languages. As a toddler, Toño watched cartoons in either language as his mother made his father breakfast following the nightshift. After brief exchanges including the code-switching of words and idiomatic phrases in Spanish and English between husband and wife, Fred would strap Toño and Sol into their car seats while speaking to them in English.

Toño's father often sang '50s tunes on the way to his mother-in-law's house when dropping off the children each morning. His grandma would wait for her grandchildren with burritos *hecho con polvo de amor*, or made with a sprinkle of love. After greeting Toño and Sol in Spanish, she would discuss the day's upcoming events with her spouse who responded alternatively between their heritage and second languages. Before rushing to work, Toño's grandpa would bounce the little *chapito* on his knee, reciting a nursery rhyme in Spanish. When the little boy cried to be put down, his *papi* would chide Toño in English.

Family, relatives, and friends noted Toño and Sol invented their own language using both English and Spanish in free play. During the day, Toño's *abuela* spoke to her *nietos* in Spanish, as did the many neighbors who stopped in for coffee. Sometimes an English-dominant aunt or older cousin would grant the gentle woman a half an hour of undisturbed housecleaning by taking Sol and Toño to the park. At sundown when Fred and Kathy exchanged a momentary conversation in between shifts, Toño's grandfather would drop off *los chiquitos* in time to kiss their mother goodbye. While their dad and uncles worked on old cars and motors in the front yard, Sol usually played with her little brother in the dirt. If the weather was too hot or cold to ride bikes or play army men, the siblings watched television and played board games until dinner and bedtime using both languages. Once Sol began elementary school, English was used more often between the brother and sister.

When it was time for Sol to attend kindergarten, the neighborhood *primaria*, Mariposa Elementary, piloted a dual-immersion program. Nervous parents who were slapped, paddled, sent to detention, or forced to eat soap for speaking Spanish learned their own children could be enrolled in a bilingual program from kindergarten through fifth grade. The parents of Gallegos were pleased to have the option of placing their five-year-olds in a learning environment where half the academic day would be taught in Spanish while the other half was instructed in English. The goal of the dual immersion program was to foster a high level of Spanish-English biliteracy in science, social studies, health and other disciplines. Memories of linguistic discrimination and forced assimilation continued to inflame Toño's family, neighbors, and friends, motivating los Galleños to enroll their children in hopes of retaining or recovering their heritage language. Under the direction of a competent and committed staff, many families viewed the use of two, unmarked school languages as a means of retaining their linguistic heritage while developing their children's intercultural and bilingual proficiencies for the global economy.

During family reunions, all eyes of the Anaya family looked proudly on young Marisol's ability to communicate, write, and translate in two languages. Toño's good-natured, intelligent sister successfully participated in the two-way bilingual program for five years, until Kathy and her fourth-grade teacher had a disagreement. The next autumn, Marisol moved in with her grandparents, enabling the child to transfer to Santa Ana Elementary's Spanish-English dual-immersion program in a different neighborhood. Her *papi* was especially excited his bright granddaughter would continue her education in both languages at school and at home.

Biliteracy Practices: Generational Tools for Personal Purposes

Conversations in the Anaya family centered around a plethora of topics. Interactions facilitating the basic routines of coming and going, eating and sleeping, working and recreating were complemented by discussions regarding individual interests and collective problem solving. A rich, oral use of Spanish and English flowed back and forth between Fred and Kathy's home into Toño's grandparents' *adobe* and back again. Distinctive family discourse topics, patterns, and structures sustained the warm, close-knit relationships among members of Toño's immediate family like an invisible, magic carpet. It was not uncommon for relatives to all speak at the same time. Members were allowed and encouraged to discuss, deliberate, or debate any idea or subject matter irrespective of age or position in the family. In conversation, the Anayas tended to speak in direct sentences, often raising their voices when emphasizing a point. The bilingual nature of this linguistic weave added to the multidimensional complexity of communications between generations.

In both homes, bits and pieces of family discourse were reflected in written text. Kathy kept an ongoing shopping list next to the personal phone book she maintained for several years. Fred collected the diagrams he drew when solving the installation of a new auto part. Before leaving home, Rudy would spend hours tracing his name in Gothic letters from examples on his record albums. Occasionally, Toño's grandpa would dictate a letter to the editor of the Spanish newspaper, *El Paisano,* that he read each morning with his coffee. His patient spouse would wait a day or two to reread and rework her husband's words into a more diplomatic response before recopying and placing the letter in the mail.

With the exception of Sol's textbooks in her pink backpack, books did not figure prominently in the Anaya family's daily routine. The written word was evidenced on commercial packaging, the television, or in the newspaper. From time to time, Fred's sister, who was a pre-school teacher, transported Sol and Toño to the city library. Although her time was limited, Fabiola always carried two or three picture books to share when it was her turn to babysit. While the sister and brother did not see their aunt more than once or twice a month, Fabiola made sure the children always had coloring books, scissors, paper, and crayons at each of the holidays. The time, effort, and example of their caring aunt set a foundation for literacy in the English language: Both Sol and Toño were able to write the majority of the letters in their names on the first day of kindergarten. When Toño was four, Fabi purchased a large photo album for Kathy and Fred's 20th wedding anniversary. The three searched the small home for piles of stray pictures. At the start of the *fiesta*, Toño could not wait for his parents to open his first real gift to them. He insisted their celebration begin by unwrapping the book of family pictures.

As the Anaya children grew older, Sol and Toño saw less of their *tía*. Like many working-class, Latino families, the responsibility for babysitting shifted to Sol as the eldest daughter. When brother and sister weren't watching television or playing outside, Marisol discovered she could use storybooks as a means to bribe Toño into behaving. The generous and wise sister checked out brightly illustrated picture books she knew her brother would enjoy when her class visited the school library once a week. In the absence of her aunt, Marisol assumed Fabi's example by modeling school behaviors and facilitating Toño's early reading and writing activities. The children amused themselves by engaging in free play, reading comic books, and scribbling in coloring books for hours while their parents completed chores or slept in between shifts. In this manner, Sol served as Toño's second and most important guide for academic language, practices, and literacy in two languages. While the siblings generally communicated in English, the devoted sister shared her textbooks, school magazines, and assignments in Spanish. Like so many older sisters, Marisol served as a first generation academic ambassador of biliteracy, feeding her demanding little brother's endless curiosity and vibrant imagination with every turn of the page. She eagerly waited for the day when Toño would start kindergarten and would eventually read by himself.

CHAPTER THREE

Beginning Kindergarten at Mariposa Elementary School

The day begins at Mariposa Elementary School long before the 8:15 bell scatters children into columns outside their classroom doors. It is still dark when the janitor flips the cheap, orange fluorescent lights to unlock a few internal doors down dark, linoleum hallways. The glow from a small lamp inside the principal's office announces her presence. She usually arrives at school before six a.m. and works most Sundays. Secretaries come into the office and lock their purses in the same desks they will be sitting in all day. The coffee pot switch is the first switch that gets flipped. It is the IV drip that maintains staff morale and vitality across the duration of the long day.

Daybreak at La Primaria / The Elementary School

Teachers appear before daylight, one by one, to haunt the ancient Xerox machine before it has a chance to break. They disappear into classrooms to round up materials for the afternoon's science experiments in order to create time for a lunch. With a recess duty and grade-level or committee meetings of some kind, most teachers will not have more than one fifteen minute break in their five or six hour day. If the educator is fortunate, her early morning preparations will be supported by one of the few knowledgeable teacher assistants remaining after budget cuts. Despite the hardship of surviving on minimum wage, these aides donate hundreds of hours of personal time before and after school.

Combating Class Warfare

Caught between a rock and a hard place, the staff and students at the *primaria* combat the realities of the urban ghetto and a political system that blames the victims of class warfare. Educators and children alike are caught in competitive crossfire between families struggling to stay alive together and a punitive state institutional system. One morning, police taped off a homicide on the street directly in front of Mariposa's main entrance. Due to a shortage in state funding, only two part-time counselors were available to meet with the children who viewed the stabbing victim on their way to school. When their *hermanos* fall ill, fourth graders remain home to care for their younger siblings so their parents won't be fired or replaced for missing one day of work. When children become sick during the school day, they sleep on the beige plastic beds of the infirmary. The school nurse will call the human resource department of their parents' employment, who won't deliver messages to workers earning minimum wage. Parents stoned on crystal meth forget to pick up their students; their children spend the remainder of the afternoon in a homeless shelter because the afterschool program has room for only thirty participants.

Unfortunately, the number of students who experience tooth pain from rotting cavities while completing state-mandated tests won't be aggregated by the state department despite its statistical challenge to the school's overall test scores. Only 4% of Mariposa's families can afford to send lunch to school with their children. Two or three times a year, the neediest students are pulled from instruction to select new shoes, pants, and a shirt from a local clothing bank. On their return, the children delight in showing off their new threads to friends at recess. During the holidays, underwear is hung from a Christmas tree outside the front office to remind visitors of the children's everyday needs year-round.

Personal and Professional Pride

And yet, a strong spirit of joy, professional commitment, and connection pervaded the hallways of Mariposa Elementary, like the scent of chocolate chip cookies the principal often baked for her staff in the teacher's lounge. The school was associated with a fierce personal and professional pride. A complicated network of professional connections, personal friendships, and familial relationships sustained and suspended the functional collaboration of the faculty. Teachers proudly asserted they would never work anywhere else. The principal spent well over a thousand dollars each year, hosting her staff to express her appreciation and counteract professional burnout.

The value placed on family, culture, and youth was visible all day, everyday in the many narratives that constituted the life of this elementary school. Unlike many institutions, this commitment was modeled by the main office. By the time the last child in line would enter their classroom to begin the instructional day, administrative assistants would have already conducted two and a half hours of business. Library materials were ordered, new students registered, and a teenage mother from the neighborhood oriented to the parent GED program. Professional development workshops were scheduled, attendance records checked, while a team of specialists considered a child's placement in special education.

The counselor assumed several professional hats. By the first bell, she would have already directed bus traffic, consoled a grieving student, and organized test booklets in an office the size of a closet. Her *jefa*, or boss, the principal, would have engaged in all sorts of activities including tracking down a missing parole officer, reviewing the resumé of a prospective substitute, and responding to twenty-five e-mails from various entities at the district office.

Community Respect, Support, and Collaboration

Both neighborhood and school cultures benefitted greatly from the historical, strategic orchestration of parental, academic, and administrative resources at Mariposa Elementary. Most community members regarded the educators with an elevated sense of respect, rarely evidenced in schools across the United States. In keeping with their Mexican-American and Mexican heritages, residents continued a long–standing tradition of ascribing authority, high culture, and wisdom to their students' teachers. In return, *las maestras* displayed a fierce commitment to addressing and providing for their students' physical, emotional, and intellectual needs. The administration and staff were held in high esteem by parents and teachers alike because of their own advocacy for the holistic development of students before, during, and after the academic day.

An Innovative, Affirming Curriculum

It is no wonder that Mariposa Elementary's emphasis on biliteracy and the multiple intelligences (Gardner, 1993) earned the school state, regional, and national recognition. The faculty's commitment to providing an innovative, affirming curriculum made the school an electric place to teach and learn. The secret to its success can be found by the school's efforts to partner with families who had been historically marginalized by the larger district. Children and parents were validated by a wide range of services including the implementation of a linguistically, culturally, and developmentally appropriate instructional program built with parent feedback. While over 90% of the 420 students at Mariposa Elementary received a free or reduced lunch, the aggregate of Spanish and English test scores indicated the children were successfully receiving a rigorous and relevant education. It was my great privilege to work for a short time with this immensely talented, passionate, and dedicated faculty. During the half year I served as a kindergarten teacher, the smell of garlic and red chile often permeated the staff room. Spanish and English echoed interchangeably with laughter in offices and classrooms. The children and teachers of Gallegos barrio, including Beto, Toño, and I were happy to come to school.

The Education of Linguistically Rich Children

The quality and type of educational services for linguistically rich children varies considerably according to the school district (Hamayan, 1990; NCES, 2003). For the most part, our educational system has reserved the goals of multilingualism and biliteracy for a small group of children. Tragically, this elite group usually does not include students from middle- and working-class families like Beto and Toño. On one end of the educational continuum, very few native English speakers participate in bilingual programs at the elementary level. At the other, middle and high school students who study "foreign languages" are rarely provided the instruction or resources to develop into balanced biliterates like their Canadian and European counterparts. To add insult to injury, most linguistically rich children are forced to relinquish their first languages (L1) and focus only on English as a second (L2) or target language during their academic career.

As we noted previously, linguistically rich children who enter school speaking a non-English language are viewed as academically and socially deficient. In viewing a child's primary home language as a cultural mismatch or academic handicap, schools have implemented inappropriate, untenable, and harmful educational prescriptions. Many linguistically rich children are simply denied essential instructional support or placed into remedial or special education programs (Hamayan, 1990; Baca and Cervantes, 2004; Halcón, 2001). In rare cases where a minimum of support is administered, the vast majority of programs seek to eliminate children's L1.

As a result, linguistically rich students earn subordinate grades, score lower on standardized tests, and drop out at higher rates (Christian, 2006). In 2007, only 17% of all Latino, Chicano, and Hispanic fourth graders were deemed proficient readers in comparison with 33% of their peers. Their eighth grade siblings did not fare much better, with only 15% scoring at or above grade level in reading (NCES, 2010). The parents of linguistically rich students often report that their child's school attendance leads to the deterioration of familial bonds among a host of other ills. Despite a corpus of legal provisions asserting their child's rights to an equal educational opportunity, the vast majority of these biliterate potentials receive very little to no academic support, thus constituting an underserved and misrepresented academic population. In contrast, Mariposa Elementary School challenged the status quo with an outstanding Two-Way Dual-Immersion, English as a Second Language, and Spanish-language instructional models, all housed in one school.

Models of Bilingual Education

Across the years, a variety of bilingual education models have been developed to address the needs of linguistically rich students. Most Americans are surprised to learn that such programs emphasize the acquisition of English as an additional language. Bilingual education models draw on over forty-five years of research from psychology, linguistics, sociology and other social sciences. These educational programs are constantly in flux, shaped by the scholarly knowledge base, political movements, and sociocultural conditions of their time. Despite a significant body of research attesting to the salience of this educational approach, the implementation of bilingual programs has been severely restricted during the past fifteen years for entrepreneurial, political, and social reasons. The three surviving forms of bilingual education in use today are distinguished by the amount of exposure to and functional use of children's primary (L1) and target languages. Transitional, maintenance, and enrichment bilingual education models facilitate differing goals for heritage, bilingual, and English-language learners.

Transitional bilingual education. The objective of transitional bilingual education (TBE) is to replace children's first language and culture with American English and norms. English as a Second Language (ESL) or English Language Development (ELD) "pull-out" programs are the most commonly implemented bilingual education model used in the United States. In this subtractive approach, linguistically rich children are removed from their regular classroom during a portion of the school day for intensive instruction in English. The curricular and instructional foci of ESL/ELD programs typically emphasizes the formal learning of English vocabulary and linguistic structures. Despite scientific research and longitudinal studies identifying this model to be the most expensive and least effective programmatic approach, ESL/ELD pull-out programs predominate the majority of bilingual education programs implemented in the United States (Crawford, 2004).

More recently, schools have moved toward Content ESL/ELD programs where linguistically rich students remain in the regular classroom to reap the psycho-sociolinguistic benefits of interaction with their native English-speaking peers. Content ESL/ELD models employ the use of trained, "push-in" educators who collaborate with regular classroom teachers to provide well-planned, specialized instruction in English. Content ESL/ELD models tap academic content from the regular curriculum, including social studies, science, health, and math to develop students' linguistic, cognitive, and academic proficiencies. Mariposa Elementary's English as a Second Language program served English language learners using a combination of push-in and pull-out services for those English language learners who were not enrolled in one of the Dual- Immersion Classrooms. In accordance with the state constitution, these children additionally received Spanish-language instruction for a small amount of time each week.

When mindfully and systematically implemented, Content ESL/ELD models employ a host of scientifically established, effective practices that can facilitate English-language acquisition (Echevarria, Vogt, and Short, 2004). Content ESL/ELD programs enable school districts to meet their minimum legal obligations to provide academic access for linguistically rich students outlined by the U.S. Supreme Court's decision in *Lau v. Nichols* (1974). However, because the students' first or home languages are not maintained or cultivated in any way, English-language acquisition can take anywhere between 5 and 10 years (Collier, 1987; Cummins, 1981; Baker, 2001).

Maintenance bilingual education. On the other hand, the goal of maintenance bilingual education (MBE) programs is to retain students' L1 while simultaneously developing English as a second or target language. Early-exit maintenance programs incorporate some use of children's native language for one to three years, while late-exit maintenance programs employ the L1 from four to eight years. For example, a district might teach Spanish-dominant children how to read and write in their first language during their first three years of school. The students would then receive literacy instruction in English in second through fifth grade. A survey of maintenance programs found that the ways in which the L1 is utilized varies widely from program to program. Very often, the majority of instructional time is actually spent in the L2. It is important to note that the maintenance model does not nurture or advance the growth of the child's L1 as a verbal or literary tool. In this manner, both transitional and maintenance models promote subtractive bilingualism. Mariposa Elementary School's bilingual program would not be characterized as a form of MBE. Instead, specific classrooms at each grade level were designated Content ESL programs with supplementary Spanish-language instruction or Two-Way, Dual-Immersion classrooms discussed below.

Enrichment bilingual education. On occasion, schools and districts have embraced enrichment bilingual education (EBE) models that deliberately combine English-dominant children and heritage, bilingual, and English-language learners. In these two-way or dual-immersion approaches, children from distinct linguistic traditions navigate the academic curriculum through both their native and target languages. In other words, all the students are language learners. It is important to note that EBE models do not employ practices involving concurrent or simultaneous translation or submersion tactics that have been found to be ineffective and potentially illegal.

Research has shown that children enrolled in EBE models have successfully appropriated essential content area knowledge while becoming proficient readers, writers, speakers, and listeners in English, Spanish, Diné (Navajo), Japanese, Chinese, Russian, and other languages (Thomas and Collier, 1997; 2002). EBE incorporate both native and second language instruction in the content areas of social studies, science, health, math, as well as language-literacy arts in both languages. The model also seeks to develop student competencies in critical literacy, intercultural communication, and technology (Faltis, 2006; Lessow-Hurley, 2009). The development of biliterate proficiencies is a central focus of the curriculum. Such models employ a sophisticated, systematic array of instructional, mediational, and evaluative measures ensuring carefully calculated immersion methods that promote positive self-esteem and additive bilingualism.

The longitudinal research of Thomas and Collier (1997; 2002) includes a multitude of findings of interest to parents, communities, and educators of linguistically rich students. Their research on various bilingual education models established that linguistically rich children who were provided with no instructional support scored in the lowest percentiles on tests, constituting the highest number of drop outs (Lindholm-Leary and Borsato, 2006). On the other hand, the researchers additionally found that, after four to seven years in a well-designed EBE program, bilingually schooled children outperformed their monolingual counterparts in all areas of academic achievement. When provided with mindful, systematic, rigorous grade-level instruction in their first and second languages, resident, native, and immigrant children challenged by low socioeconomic conditions scored at high levels on academic tests in their target or second language (Thomas and Collier, 2002).

Subsequent studies by researchers including Lindholm-Leary and Borsato (2006) concur with these results, noting "strong convergent evidence that the educational success of English language learners is positively related to sustained instruction through the students' first language" (p. 201). Linguistically diverse students attributed EBE programs as a major deterrent to dropping out of school prior to graduation (Thomas and Collier, 2002; Lindholm-Leary and Borsato, 2006). A direct correlation exists between the length of stay in EBE programs and greater positive outcomes specific to reading and math achievement, grade point average, attendance, high school completion rates, attitudes toward school, and attitudes towards the self (Lindholm-Leary and Borsato, 2006). To date, two-way or dual-immersion models remain the only programs enabling linguistically rich children to score at the 50th percentile or higher on achievement tests administered in both their first and second languages (Thomas & Collier, 2002). In other words, TBE programs remain the only educational approach scientifically proven to bridge the achievement gap for linguistically diverse students in the United States. When implemented through high-quality, well-designed policies and practices, the goal of biliteracy produces a myriad of benefits for both linguistically rich children and their English-dominant peers.

Challenges to a Smooth Induction into School

Fortunately, the Chavez and Ortiz-Anaya families had access to a high-quality, dual-immersion program at Mariposa Elementary School. The boys' induction into the formal education system, however, was not without its bureaucratic challenges. After a much-anticipated surge in enrollment left up to thirty-five children in three separate kindergartens, state and district authorities finally permitted the principal to hire an additional, full-time kindergarten teacher forty days after the first day of school. Establishing a new section of kindergarten resulted in the redistribution of over a hundred five-and six-year-olds into four distinct classrooms. However, as several credible sources had predicted, new students continued to enroll after October first, making it necessary to hire an additional half-time teacher.

Due to a state-created teacher shortage, very few candidates were left to fill the half-time kindergarten position. A full-time substitute with a bachelor's degree in secondary social studies education was hired to work with an overflow of twelve kindergarteners. After a month or so, Mariposa's principal began to search for the subsitute's replacement because the woman was unkind to the five-year-olds. The limited amount of instruction the substitute had provided was not developmentally appropriate or relevant to preparing the children for first grade. When I took over the small class in mid–December, I was either the third or fourth teacher the children had been introduced to in four and a half months.

Limited funds from the state prevented the district and school from providing the children and their families with an all-day kindergarten. As a result, our half-time kindergarten class met for two and a half hours together each morning. Aside from our work in Spanish and English literacy and numeracy, the kindergarteners also attended physical education, library, recess and lunch in accordance with state law. Let's return now to Beto and Toño's families to get a glimpse of how the two little boys transitioned into kindergarten as well as my initial impressions of each of these unique, linguistically rich children.

Beto Begins Kindergarten

Beto's induction into the formal educational system was complicated by larger bureaucratic structures, policies and lack of vision that devalue children in our society. In contrast, his transition into kindergarten was wholly supported in his home life. As we saw in Beto's home, immigrant families understand first-hand, the value of a good education. His father, older brother, and *padrino* all expressed pride when the little boy began kindergarten. Juana and Miranda organized Beto's breakfast, clothes, shoes, and backpack each morning. The fortunate child started each school day listening to the expectations of his mother and two older sisters on the way to school. Juana and Miranda reappeared at lunch time and were often accompanied by Beto's aunt and younger cousin. During these visits, the family hoped little Lily might become accustomed to what kindergarten would be like in the following year. Beto was reminded a strong and loving family awaited him at the start and end of every school day.

This familial support proved essential for the young boy to adapt to four separate teachers across four and a half months' time. Juana's care for Beto provided a consistent structure and routine amidst a critical introduction into a chaotic school culture. In spite of so many novelties and changes, Beto attended kindergarten regularly and missed class only on days when illness prevented his attendance. Juana regularly consulted with Beto's teachers, rescued papers from his backpack, and, with the help of her eldest daughter's writing skills, submitted important documents to the school when necessary. Her concern to establish a safe, secure, and supportive experience for her son overshadowed her own feelings of discomfort in what can be a confusing and novel environment. The high value Juana and Eduardo placed on *respeto, modales, y trabajo* were reflected in Beto's kindness, manners, and effort in class. Indeed, at the end of the school year, the Chavez family's youngest child received several awards for good citizenship and academic achievement.

First Impressions of Beto in December

The children were seated in groups of four around circular tables. As I walked around the tiny classroom where I would be teaching kindergarten, I noticed two little boys sitting close together talking under their breath. The two children were faced with a pile of tattered magazines. One child held a torn page in his hands, while his *amiguito* cut out a picture from a separate page.

I reached over the table's edge to introduce myself. Both boys immediately stopped whispering and sat up straight in their chairs. They each slightly bowed their chins and turned their black-brown eyes down and away to the side. Avoiding eye contact, I told them my name and asked what they were doing in Spanish. The sound of cutting paper was the only response I received. I complimented the boys on their work and began to walk away. The boy with the scissors continued cutting with his face directed at the table. His companion stole a quick glimpse up at me through long, black eyelashes. As I returned the look with a smile, his eyes quickly darted away. In many traditional Mexican families, the child's avoidance of direct eye contact denotes a sign of respect for adult authority.

I circulated the room and chatted with the substitute teacher. She identified the little boys as Francisco and Roberto. I found out later she had called Umberto by the wrong name for two months. Based on the children's behavior, I also suspect she banned the use of Spanish in the tiny classroom. Before exiting the room, I returned to the boys' table to say goodbye. The children were working so intently, their two heads almost touched as they carefully glued pictures to a common paper. Umberto looked up and, this time, I nodded gently and smiled warmly at his face. He immediately glanced down to the side again to show his respect. I walked to the door and turned to wave goodbye. Umberto's head turned and his eyes searched out mine for an instant. Upon meeting, he beamed me a hopeful, half-smile, and quickly returned to his task.

Toño Starts Kindergarten

As kindergarten registration approached, the Anayas decided to enroll Toño at Santa Ana Elementary in his grandparents' neighborhood. The placement would have allowed Fred and Kathy greater flexibility in child care. Because the school was located within walking distance of their adobe, Toño's grandma could drop off and pick up both her *nietos* when full-day kindergarten was dismissed. As a fourth grader, Sol would be on-site in the event her little brother was sick, injured, or bullied at school. The Anaya family was also eager for Toño to participate in recovering their family's linguistic heritage in an all-day, dual-immersion Spanish-English kindergarten.

However, things went differently than originally planned. The shift from home to school cultures proved problematic for Toño. A highly sensitive and willful child, Toño was used to getting his way or having his attention diverted by relatives. Within a larger power dynamic, common behavior expectations proved to be a source of tension for the young child. Without the experience of pre-school, Toño was overwhelmed by the length of the school day. He also did not adjust well to a full schedule of activities in academic Spanish. After several screaming tantrums, Toño's first kindergarten teacher recommended the exhausted child be transferred to a half-day program.

In the half-time Spanish kindergarten at Santa Ana, Toño's angry fits continued. He did not associate the language of his grandmother's kitchen with the academic Spanish of the classroom. Within a few weeks, Toño's second teacher suggested the child be placed in an English-dominant, half-day kindergarten closer to home. At the start of the second grading period in October, Fred and Kathy enrolled their son at Mariposa Elementary approximately three miles from his parent's home.

The switch to Toño's neighborhood school did not turn out to be a smooth transition either. Toño's third kindergarten teacher was a kind and enthusiastic woman who was hired a week after the start of the school year. Toño's personal contact with her was limited as the educator attempted to induct thirty five and six-year-olds into the school culture without a teacher's assistant. Upon his transfer into a smaller class, the little boy's tantrums before and during school sharply increased. Without any formal training in developmental psychology or early childhood education, the substitute teacher banished Toño to the hallway on a regular basis. When other students began imitating his fits, Toño was abruptly disciplined and sent home. In December, I replaced this educator to become Toño's fifth kindergarten teacher in five months.

Toño's induction into the educational system was further complicated when the family car broke down in early November. Fred and Kathy's work schedule depended on seamless, back-to-back transitions between their day and evening shifts. A few months' savings were required to purchase a new alternator. Because their home was only one mile from Mariposa Elementary, the school district did not provide bus transportation for the children living on Toño's street. After an eight-hour shift of physically demanding labor, Kathy would be confronted by a kicking, screaming, tearful Toño who refused to walk to school in the cold. There were no facilities Kathy might frequent that would allow her to sleep on campus. Therefore, the struggling mother was required to make two one-mile trips on foot between home and school in order for Toño to receive two hours of kindergarten instruction each day.

A pattern of two to three absences per week was well established by the end of November. On many of the days Toño did come to school between

January and May, he arrived up to an hour and a half late. Tensions heightened between Kathy and administrators legally obligated to refer excessive absences to the municipal children's court. By the end of January, Kathy appeared before a judge twice for educational neglect. Despite my positive relationship with the family, routines held steadfast in the Anaya household. In the spring, the school counselor threatened to fine the family $50.00 for every day Toño was absent. Between mid-December and late May, Toño was tardy seventeen times and absent forty days.

First Impressions of Toño in December

I had taught six school days before Toño bounced into our kindergarten classroom. "Teacher, teacher! Teacher, teacher!" shouted a spry, tiny boy in English. The child turned in circles, waving his hands in the air. "Teacher, teacher!" he shouted again. "I'm back!"

Toño stopped abruptly, peered out of one green eye and informed me, "You're not teacher!" In a rapid glance around him, Toño noticed the room had been changed around. "Hey! Magazines!" he yelled.

I put down the book I had been reading to Beto and his classmates at my feet. A girl announced in a dry voice, "That's Toño. He doesn't come much."

Toño rifled through the periodicals I had set in our library at lightning speed. He opened a magazine, pointed to the pictures, giggled loudly, turned a few pages, and moved on to the next magazine in the display. By the time he finished flipping through a second Ranger Rick science magazine, I intercepted him at the bookcase. "Come sit down with us," I urged, taking his hand. "We're reading a story."

"Wait—no! I write my name!" the child insisted.

Toño tore out of my grasp, rushing to the morning sign-in chart. He proceeded to write his full name in capital letters while lip-synching the sound of each letter in Spanish. Using his left hand, Toño wrote from right to left. When he reached the last letter o in his name, the child leaned as close to the table as he could without touching his cheekbone. He proceeded to draw a tiny face in the center of the last letter. Then, in one graceful movement, Toño lifted his head, stood up, leaned back, surveyed his work with satisfaction, and pulled the marker cap off his tongue. The plastic piece made a popping noise that sounded like a chuckle. Toño's eyes widened with delight. He cocked his head to one side and exclaimed, "Hey!" Pulling the cap from his mouth, the little boy examined the object with a newfound respect.

Braiding a Pedagogical Path

My first encounters with Toño and Beto offered a telling snapshot of each little boy's personality, learning style, and emergent biliterate proficiencies. Over the course of the next nine months, the children would blossom into emergent listeners, speakers, readers and writers of Spanish and English. As their teacher, I, too, would undergo my own crash course in education. In order to guide the boys over the threshold of literacy, at the macro level, I would have to combine my own pedagogical knowledge with the institutional goals and effective practices adopted by Mariposa Elementary School. At the micro level, I would need to become literate about the minds and hearts of the boys and their families to design a relevant and meaningful curriculum for them. I would grapple with moments of laughter, crying, and the gnashing of teeth. As the newcomer to Beto and Toño's classroom, I would draw on a host of resources to braid this pedagogical path for all of us. Let's take a quick peek to see how this was done.

CHAPTER FOUR

A Half Day in Our Bilingual Classroom

White light streamed down a narrow hallway obscured by dark, dancing silhouettes. The outlines of one flying plane, two trumpeting elephants, and four super heroes engaged in mortal combat slowly took shape as Charlene and I raced into the glare.

Shoes squeaking, we quickly advanced down the hall, and the noise from the cluster of moving characters grew louder. Stopping abruptly, I requested, "Boys, please, stand still." A puddle began to form where Charlene and I waited, holding hands.

"Please," I implored the group of children. "Please stop, and get in line."

Other classes navigated slowly in perfect file around us with the silent efficiency of well-trained ghosts; teachers urged their students to "keep walking and look away" in irritated whispers. We had completely upset the multi-grade, pre-lunch bathroom routine of eight classrooms. Seemingly oblivious to everything around them, my boys continued to dive bomb, stampede, joust and cut off heads, captured by their imaginations.

I pushed down the urge to panic. Taking a deep breath, I loudly asserted in a kind but firm voice, "Stop talking and stand in line, RIGHT...NOW."

The eight kindergarteners stopped in their tracks, staring at me in blank, innocent surprise. All at once, I understood everything.

My First Week of Kindergarten

It was the third day since I had taken over my tiny class of nine kindergarteners. Like Monday and Tuesday, we were already way off schedule. Transitioning the children from one activity to another had been a constant struggle, leaving me to exhaustedly wonder if I would be better at herding cats. During our Wednesday fifteen-minute bathroom break, Charlene had lathered her cheeks, hands, and full arms with so much soap she had been unable to shut off the thundering faucet, flooding the entire bathroom. As the boys and I had waited for the tiny girl and her friend, Isabella returned, softly reporting that her classmate needed help. Instructing the class to wait in line quietly, I dashed into the girl's bathroom to find Charlene stuck in the mouth of the sink, with her tippy-toes dangling precariously mid-air. In the short period of time it took to dislodge, rinse, and dry her off, my class had technically been without adult supervision for four minutes. Four minutes was enough time for a flying machine to begin dropping missles over small cities. It was sufficient for bull elephants to charge each other with fearsome white tusks, trumpeting through the bush. And it was enough time for my personal group of action figures to resume a make-believe but potentially fatal swordfight from yesterday's recess.

This was not the first time I had experienced the youthful exuberance of primary students unfamiliar with academic culture. A veteran elementary teacher of eight years, my first graders in Colorado had also not known how to line up for lunch on their very first day. Similarly, my second, fourth, and fifth grade students from rural Chihuahua often needed explicit instructions regarding the expectations and practices of American schools. But somehow, as I stood before my tiny class, I realized *this was different*. All week, I had used every trick in the book to engage and redirect the small children to no avail. As the puddle below Charlene and I swelled into a small pond, I suddenly realized why the previous teacher had been released for constantly yelling at the children: she had not known to teach them basic school behaviors.

Observing in the Substitute's Classroom

My observations and interactions prior to assuming the class had been rather disturbing. The trailer was filthy and reeked of pidgeon and mouse feces. Hundreds of stacks of worksheets gathered dust waiting silently in all corners of the classroom. Without a set of hooks, the kindergarteners' coats were strewn across the floor; children tripped over backpacks scattered in the play area. Close inspection of a group of papers revealed the substitute's attempts at teaching cursive writing before print. Her lesson plans noted only one story had been read to the children in thirty days. Mathematics was not incorporated into the daily curriculum, relegated as a parental responsibility through nightly homework. The English directions on these worksheets were unreadable to the majority of Spanish-speaking families. Despite a small number of toys and a used kitchen set that took up half the total classroom space, choice or self-selection time was permitted only on Fridays for those students who had been well behaved across the five-day week.

A typical morning in the substitute's kindergarten began with the ABC song in English. Next, Toño and Beto's peers would complete three daily worksheets. The substitute read the directions to all three worksheets at the same time. The children were left to complete the work independently as she sat at her desk. The first three of the nine kinders to correctly complete all of their papers won a piece of candy.

On a day I observed, one of the worksheet themes centered around the question, "What do we put in our backpacks?" The Spanish-dominant class was told in English to distinguish between the pictures of school supplies and household items. Examples were not provided, nor did any discussion take place that would allow the five-year-olds to model from or think through the selection process required to find an answer. Student choices were then colored, cut, and pasted to the top of a large backpack in the middle of the page. Upon hearing instructions to this particular worksheet, a trilingual child sighed loudly and whined, "We *always* color-cut-paste!" Wisely, none of the children selected the glue bottle when finishing their assignment. This intelligent omission was later circled as a mistake in red pen.

Even art followed a similar diet of meaningless activities. One day, I observed as a child was provided an orange piece of construction paper and instructed to cut and paste orange magazine items onto the field. The intention behind the activity was to review color words and items. However, the stack of political magazines available to the children were disheveled and picked over from months of use. I watched in horror as one of Beto and Toño's classmates expressed great delight in finally finding something orange after fishing through three shredded magazines. The child smiled broadly while pasting a photo of a corpse from the Bosnian war that happened to be clad in an orange dress.

These examples serve to illustrate the fact that the boys' early school activities were developmentally, linguistically, and academically inappropriate. In her defense, the substitute had been trained as a high school social studies teacher. Like many people with limited study and experience working with young children, she embraced the common, ageist opinion that kindergarten was "all fun and games" because she "didn't have to teach reading." The primary grades are a hotbed of psycho-sociolinguistic development that, as other countries observe, need to be staffed by professionals with sophisticated expertise.

Performing School Culture: Beginning at the Beginning

I was drawn out of my reverie in the hall way to the immediacy of the task at hand. My kindergarteners were not performing school culture by forming lines, standing quietly, or washing their hands without taking a bath. The substitute had either not known or had failed to teach the students simple educational protocols. After all, *this was kindergarten*. In a flash of light, the enormity of the task was infinitely clear: we needed to begin at the beginning.

The appropriation of a behavioral curriculum became the focus of our first few weeks together. Together, the children and I established our daily routine, school practices, "indoor" responses and academic behaviors through games, songs, positive reinforcement, imaginative role-play, preventative discipline and praise. Time, modeling and feedback were needed to organize and establish joint attention, turn-taking, and egalitarian power dynamics that lay the foundation for shared literacy events. These relational structures provided the groundwork for a process approach to biliteracy. It was necessary to take the time to build relationships with the kindergarteners and their families to inspire, shape, and internalize positive behavior choices. For some of the children, this was the first instance when public and private behaviors were distinguished between their homes and the outside world. Foundational knowledge, strategies, skills, and dispositions became the rock upon which our collective curriculum and personal school success was built. By the end of the month, I was convinced that if there really was an afterlife, an area that looked like the Hilton on Maui should be reserved specifically for kindergarten teachers.

Constructing the Curriculum

A Creative Process and Artifact

Constructing a curriculum is much like the tailoring of a fine garment. Its fabric must be woven from a variety of sources in order to ensure its quality, strength, and beauty. After the cloth is measured and cut, major sections are stitched together to form its basic shape. Draping the clothing over a model, the seamstress will then engage in a dance of examining and sewing, critiquing and adjusting between her informed eyes and skillful hands. Designing our kindergarten curriculum was an ongoing process that never was never truly complete. The children's responses, needs, and interests often dictated where our fabric needed gathering and tucking or loosening and securing. Colleagues observed the creative process to make suggestions and contribute piecework or embroidery. For example, a reading specialist came into our class once a week to teach a specific phonics curriculum adopted by the school. Feedback from my administrators' formal and informal observations helped me to place details on my instruction or modify pragmatic uses of the curriculum itself. This dynamic process resulted in a curricular artifact crafted for its dual capacity to protect and adorn.

The Institution and Official Knowledge

In order to construct a well-rounded, wholistic curriculum, I first conducted an analysis of the state and district standards outlined for kindergarteners at Mariposa Elementary School. These documents collectively represented the bare-bones, "official curriculum" or institutional knowledge designated for student learning at kindergarten. Because our founding fathers relegated education to be the responsibility of individual states, it was important for me to examine how Colorado's primary curriculum differed from that of my new home state. In reviewing state and district standards, I looked for places where the learning objectives were smoothly aligned or dramatically differed. Hypothetically, district standards should reflect and refine those objectives adopted by the state. However, across the course of my career, I have discovered that curricular reciprocity is few and far between, being dependent on the vision and leadership of mid-level district administrators and state department of education officials.

I then compared my analysis with Mariposa Elementary School's mission statement, report card, and other documents that formalized learning expectations and student behavior for children attending Mariposa Elementary. In this case, the foresight and expertise of my colleagues must be commended in that the Kindergarten Developmental Progress Record (KDPR), originally designed to monitor student progress, additionally served as the grade report. Again, most districts do not possess such a high degree of curricular and evaluative alignment. Nor do their assessments reflect the expertise of professional associations like the International Reading Association (IRA), Teachers of English to Students of Other Languages (TESOL), or the National Association of the Education of Young Children (NAEYC). As a result, these assessments often include outrageous learning objectives producing disasterous results with tragic educational implications. Happily, the professional knowledge offered by these organizations was reflected in the KDPR used to evaluate Toño, Beto, and their classmates.

A Closer Look at the Kindergarten Report Card

The assessment/report card was classified into three parts described as socio-affective, physical, and intellectual development. Intellectual development was further divided into sections for visual arts and music; science, health, and safety; social studies, mathematics, and the language arts. These areas were further broken down into learning objectives related to basic academic behaviors, literacy, and numeracy. For example, the test measured how well a student could share or work in small groups, identify basic colors and parts of the body, associate the numerals 1-10 with the correct quantity, and match upper- and lowercase letters across three grading periods. The document indicated whether a child's performance on these criteria "met essential achievement," was characterized as "beginning: need[ing] more time or experience,"or was designated as an area of "need". It was expected that kindergarteners would be proficient in these majority of criteria to be advanced to first grade by May.

School Expectations

In addition to the KDPR, Mariposa Elementary's kindergarten and first grade teams had prioritized a list of twenty essential skills to take precedence over other criteria. In some instances, this document replicated district and state curriculum including learning objectives such as name, color, shape, number, and letter recognition or the ability to recite one's full name, address, phone number or birthday. The vast majority of these items required basic recognition and rote memorization tasks. In other instances, Mariposa Elementary's Twenty Skill List included strategic or procedural knowledge that promoted personal independence and responsibility such as the ability to tie one's shoes or zip up a coat. In short, I prioritized this official knowledge and compared it to a comprehensive portrait of class needs to establish key targets for curriculum, instruction, and assessment. This collective information structured the zone of proximal development between the kindergarteners proficiency levels in December and that which they would eventually achieve with assistance.

Mariposa Elementary School's vision, mission and program goals were equally important to review. Faculty and staff worked collaboratively with families and other care-providers to produce graduates who were "bilingual, biliterate, and competent in all academic areas." In order to achieve this accomplishment, the faculty implemented "strong academic programs designed to motivate and challenge students and enhance language competencies in English and Spanish" using the district core curriculum, state standards, collaborative curricular design, and ongoing assessment of children "on a consistent, on-going basis for reading, writing, and math." All full-day programs participated in a uninterrupted literacy/biliteracy block for two to two and a half hours per day. Dual-immersion classrooms that met for the full-day implemented instruction "in both Spanish and English using a 50/50model in grades 1–5 and a 90/10 model in kindergarten.

Teachers, adminstrators, faculty, and staff were committed to the following program goals: to realize high academic achievement; to promote bilingualism and biliteracy; to develop a high sense of self-esteem, positive attitude, and strong identity; to develop cross-cultural thoughtfulness; and to foster a proactive community that advocates for our programs and education. Instructional models included discovery and cooperative learning; whole language instruction; critical thinking skills development; an integrated curriculum; multicultural thoughtfulness; phonetic instruction; and parental involvement.

Family Goals and Objectives

A second source for our curriculum came from the children's parents and caregivers. After distributing a letter of introduction, I met with members of each family to solicit their perceptions of and hopes and dreams for their students' school success. Experience has taught me these guardians hold very definite aspirations for their children. Regardless of educational, economic, or cultural background, when given an opportunity to voice their ambitions in an atmosphere of respect, family members can make insightful and meaningful contributions to the construction of the curriculum. Both Beto and Toño's parents responded favorably to voicing educational objectives for their sons. Our informal conferences extended across the remainder of the year, into the summer as a shared, reciprocal effort on behalf of the boys.

The Emotional Curriculum

There is an additional component to the construction of the curriculum often neglected in discussions regarding student learning and achievement. While scholars have correctly distinguished between the official and unofficial curriculum (see Banks; Apple, etc.) a socio-affective dimension is always invisibly woven beside or into cognitive objectives. The emotional curriculum is derived from the lived experience of children; their construction of identity in their private and public lives; the response, affection, and meaning they assign to teachers, classmates, and school; and both their individual and collective feelings of agency. It is essential for teachers to actively and mindfully address and positively extend these aspects of children's psychological realities by cultivating a positive environment with joyful venues to develop academic confidence. Ultimately, it is the emotional curriculum that girds student learning. A powerful sense of worth, care, and resilience are necessary to sustain the repeated risktaking inherent in the learning process, as surely as novice acrobats require a safety net below them.

Deliberately interweaving a positive emotional curriculum was especially important for my tiny kindergarten class. All nine children were struggling individually with the impact of living with adult-sized issues. Their comments, stories, and behaviors related lived experiences of divorce and abandonment, drug and alcohol addiction, discrimination and prejudice, physical and sexual abuse, death and murder as well as eviction and homelessness. Because the ability of their parents and caregivers to combat the effects of these social problems was limited due to severely restricted finances, it was not uncommon for the children to resort to inappropriate responses that sometimes complicated our instructional sessions. In the beginning, we often needed to stop and address these behaviors as learning opportunities with better choices to ensure short- and long-term school success. For example, one child had spent the first five years of his life living in a van. His mother, father, and three siblings resided at various truck stops in the area. Because he had never lived in an apartment, trailer or house, he did not have a sense of interpersonal space or independent possession of material items. To ignore his grabbing, hitting, and pushing behaviors would have been an invitation for the rest of the class to engage in similar choices.

Therefore, we collectively worked in social studies on taking turns, asking for permission, and ways to include oneself or make space for others. Martin Luther King Day offered the chance to further discuss issues of equality and respect, while practicing anti-bullying actions. By Valentine's Day, we were actively implementing friendship-building strategies by deliberately issuing compliments, apologies, and other polite discourse. Across the course of five months, each individual student worked toward polishing a personal aspect of the emotional curriculum that was especially meaningful to him or her. Isabella would learn to write letters to her father, who lived out of state, when she missed him. The school counselor met once a week with Charlene for grief counseling. Jorge and his mother implemented a reward program to motivate him to complete his homework based on the system we used in class; this practice offset the verbal and physical battering he received for enjoying his school work and "acting like a girl" from his father and older brothers. Toño practiced crunching his toes and counting to ten in two languages instead of kicking someone. His friend John discovered the safest place to sit in the car when his father drove home drunk. Children's sorrows enter the classroom dynamic through their interactions, choicemaking, art and play. One of the greatest gifts we can give to our students is a safe, healthy space where protective choices, self-soothing practices, and cathartic opportunities constitute the emotional curriculum, while promoting children's health, agency and school success.

Curricular Resources and Constraints: Instructional Materials and Schedules

Two additional sources shaped our resulting curriculum. First, the availability of developmentally, culturally, and linguistically appropriate materials impacted the thematic units we explored. These essential items are the raw materials from which teachers and children internalize the curriculum, including multiple copies of children's literature, math manipulatives, art reproductions, poetry posters, and field trip monies. As the failure of the subsitute's worksheet-based approach suggested, without access to a variety of these critical instructional supports, meaningful learning is hard pressed to occur.

Second, our monthly and daily schedule defined the class explorations to a significant extent. After a typical period of transition and assessment coupled by the holiday season, Beto and Toño's classmates and I had only five solid months together until the end of school in May; we had a great deal to accomplish in a short amount of time. There was no denying that the system had set up the children for retention. Therefore, in conjunction with the school's marking periods, I set tentative benchmarks, deadlines, and due dates in which to gauge student success and implement our instructional units of study. Our weekly schedule was additionally confounded by the state's refusal to provide funding for a full day of kindergarten. Therefore, we met Mondays through Fridays from 8:20 to 11:15 on the days school was in session. This three-hour time slot included a daily lunch from 10:30 to 10:55 a.m. each day. We began transitioning to lunch at 10:20 in order to be in the cafeteria line without holding up the classes that were served behind us. As the children ate quietly, we reviewed numbers, letters, parts of the body, names of food items, and conversational dialogue in English and Spanish. From 11:00 to 11:15, we were responsible for clearing our trays and washing down tables and seats. We also used this transition time to pass out papers, zipper up backpacks, put on coats, and connect with parents, programs, and other caregivers. Anyone who has had the joy of placing one five-year-old into a snowsuit will appreciate the difficulties with this schedule with nine children.

Once the lunch hour was deducted from our day, our instructional time was further reduced by a daily fifteen-minute journey into the main building for a bathroom break. Individual kindergarteners were not allowed to run across the courtyard to use the bathroom by themselves. The children also attended physical education and library once a week for thirty minutes a session. Gratefully, these essential classes supported our main objectives set for school behaviors, numeracy, and literacy. In the end, while the children attended school fifteen hours per week, only a little over four and a half hours of instructional time were available to us during that time. In other words, Beto and Toño's classmates and I only met for two fifty-five- and three eighty-five- minute instructional sessions each week. This amount of time was not sufficient for the curriculum coverage necessary for school success, resulting in the retention of several students' at year's end. Needless to say, I became an avid proponent of pre-school and all-day kindergarten early in my teaching assignment.

In order to satisfy state requirements for Spanish-language instruction and prepare the children for the dual-immersion program, after the New Year, I adopted a 50/50 approach where we alternated the use of Spanish and English every other day. By no means would I characterize this approach as a full-fledged dual-immersion program. However, given the limited number of instructional minutes we had each day, it was the best and most equitable way to meet the needs of our tiny class.

Units of Investigation with Instructional Themes

With a solid understanding of state, district, and school objectives and the materials and amount of time we had to accomplish them with, I then organized the curriculum into three instructional themes. In addition to holiday and special events like the children's birthdays, the topics "All About Me," "My Home, My Community," and "Animals, Animals, and More Animals" allowed us to explore, appropriate, and internalize discrete aspects of the curriculum in a cyclical, integrated, and meaningful manner. For example, the district required the students to know their whole name, phone number, address, and birthday. However, on Mariposa Elementary's List of Twenty Skills, name recognition was prioritized as the first and most important item. Actually *writing* one's first and last name were indicated as the ninth and tenth most important skills, while reciting and writing home address and phone number were registered as numbers fifteen and sixteen respectively. However, there is a huge distinction in the psycho-sociolinguistic proficiencies required to recognize, recite, and write basic information. By sequencing instructional themes in a developmental manner, the teaching-learning process allowed the children to move from oral to written representations of knowledge as they studied themselves, their families, school, and communities, as well as the natural world.

The progression of our units of investigation also afforded the opportunity to differentiate or meet, greet, and extend the children's current level of proficiencies with targeted instruction. For example, as Patrick learned to recite his address and phone number by heart, he was also mastering the procedural strokes for writing numbers. In mid-winter, he was able to independently address a letter to himself that was mailed at the local post office. The boy enjoyed learning visual representations for quantity from dice, quickly transferring number sense to counting play money. Toward the end of the year, Patrick enjoyed informing his classmates how much items cost in the local newspaper; his understanding of numbers and mathematics had qualitatively transformed over time. Constructing the curriculum in this manner provided the developmental space for Toño, Beto and their classmates to be exposed to, discover, experience, and eventually internalize discrete elements of the curriculum in a meaningful context. Like the spokes on a bike wheel, the processes of speaking, listening, reading and writing in two languages collectively centered on a thematic hub. At the opposite end, these spokes supported the larger wheel of biliteracy transporting Beto, Toño, and their peers to novel epistemological and imaginative spaces as we witness in the next chapter. But first, let's walk through a typical day in late February with our boys.

A Half Day in Our Bilingual Kindergarten Classroom

Ven Acá: Come on Over

The shrill of the second bell is accompanied by shrieks of laughter and the patter of six hundred feet dash into lines. Outside the off-white trailer, Toño, Beto, and their classmates line up on the wooden ramp leading into our side of the trailer. Heaving open the heavy fire door, I greet our class with a smile, high five or pat on the shoulder, wishing each student, "Good morning" as they stream past me in our designated language for the day.

The kindergarteners march through the narrow foyer, entering our tiny room. We can hear the muffled sounds of the special education class next door as another colleague begins the school day. Over the weekend, our small space has been vacuumed and aired out. Charlene dramatically breathes in the fresh vanilla scent from a new room deodorizer exclaiming, "It smells like cookies in here."

A large white erase board hangs at the far end of the rectangular room, flanked by a teacher's desk and small computer station in the right hand corner. A row of bookcases and supply tables stand against the wall to the left. Word walls categorized by letters and corresponding terms and pictures decorate each side of the trailer at the children's height. Isabella walks over to finger a new postcard in Spanish while Patrick runs to the opposite side of the room, scanning the English side for the lexical equivalent.

Eventually, the kindergarteners parade to the coat hooks located at the near end of the right-hand corner by the play area, hanging their backpacks and jackets. Carlitos glances at the label below his hook, whispering the word "jacket" as he associates the label with a picture of a coat under his name. He takes great care to make sure the outerwear won't fall where Isa and Char will step on it when playing house. A small wooden kitchenette is sectioned off by milk crates stuffed with games, toys, puzzles, and puppets for later in the morning.

"Ven acá," Toño urges. "Come on over here." The friendly boy calls you to the small cluster of square and round tables occupying the middle of the space.

"We always sign in here," he adds, pointing to the clipboard with the date, month, and year written in the language of the day. Several children before you have already written their names. Sergio's signature includes his full first and last name, written in block print. John has indicated his presence by carefully drawing his first initial below it. Grandma Mela, a local volunteer, circulates, gently reminding each child to turn their *tarea* into the homework box and mark if they will be eating cold or hot lunch on our calendar with a blue or red slip.

While I read a note from Patrick's grandpa and Isa runs the attendance and lunch count to the front office, the children select a text to read independently on the carpet, against a pillow, or at a table. "Ven acá," encourages Carlitos, beckoning you to select from the read-aloud books; children's periodicals; predictable texts; and ABC, counting, or picture books displayed on the bookcase. "We can sit here together," he adds, patting a pillow for you to sit down.

By the time school-wide announcements start, Isa has returned from the office and begun silently mouthing the words to the same picture book she reads every single morning. Next to her, John has selected, *Big Fish, Little Fish*, and is supplying one-word statements about the plot as he points to each picture. As he enthusiastically turns each page, John's vocabulary echoes the exact text I used when reading the book to the class just yesterday.

Raising my hand to give the silent signal, I walk over to Patrick to catch his eye. I tap my right ear and shake my head at the same time, indicating that I can't hear the principal speaking over his giggling. When I turn my back, Toño sticks out his tongue at Patrick and Sergio points to the second rule on the board that reads, "Escuchamos a la maestra" and "We listen to the teacher."

The voice over the loudspeaker blares that it is time for the pledge. "Stand up, please," I state while indicating for the children to rise with an upswing of both my hands. The kindergarteners imitate me as I walk toward the flag and place my right hand over my heart. With my left hand, I point to each word from the chart on the wall as we recite:

> "Juro fidelidad a la bandera de los Estados Unidos
> de America. Y a la republica que representa una nación,
> bajo Dios, indivisible, con libertad y justicia para todos."

After the pledge is recited a second time in English, the front office concludes announcements by wishing everyone a good day. I clap my hands two times and declare that I will need everyone's help because we are running a little behind for Calendar and Weather Station. The children fan out to return their books and sit at the foot of a large easel in front of the white board. Dragging my chair beside the chart paper, I glance over to Toño who has been distracted by a book about scorpions and state calmly, "Ven acá, mijo." I move a card with his name from the green to the yellow lens of a large traffic light on the front board, signaling he has made a choice that might prevent him from the privilege of self-selection time later in the morning. He quickly closes the book and makes a beeline for John.

Recognizing this is also not an optimal choice for the active little boy, Grandma Mela kneels down at the back of the class and taps the space next to her saying, "Ven aquí." The kindergartener backtracks his steps to sit beside her as John sits up a little taller, looking at the easel with a serious face.

During our everyday ritual, we identify the month, date, and year. After singing a song about the days of the week in order, we identify today as Wednesday, the twelfth day of February. We also establish the day and dates for yesterday and tomorrow. Examining the base ten patterns inherent in our calendar, we engage in mental math by calculating how many more days of school before Valentine's Day.

These basic addition and subtraction problems continue into the weather report after John and Patrick check the sky and temperature, publicly relating and recording their observations with numerals and other figurative symbols, also on the calendar. I encourage everyone to make a prediction for tomorrow's weather, casually asking Isabella to translate John's forecast into the language of the day so he can repeat it to the larger group.

All at once, Beto raises his hand urgently. He points to the window, indicating that it is snowing outside, Grandma Mela and I exchange glances with a mischievous smile. Agreeing aloud that we need examine weather patterns in the field like real television anchors, we hurriedly collect our coats and line up at the door. The children urge straggling classmates, "Ven acá!" before their teachers change their minds.

Outside, we race around the playground in near blizzard conditions as thick, fluffy flakes adorn our lashes and hair. We talk about how clouds form and practice using the word precipitation. Carlitos and Beto are encouraged to think about how they will report this weather activity tomorrow. Sergio starts a game to see how many snowflakes he can catch and his *compañeros* join him willingly. He advises you to use his personal technique of cradling the flakes inside his cupped hands. Opening his palms and pointing to the moisture on his skin, I note that the snowflakes have changed from solids to liquids like we discussed last week in science. We laugh at the thought of frying snowflakes in a pan to make a gas or steam before he runs off to explain his discovery to Beto and Sergio.

By now, it is almost time for our bathroom break, so we quench our thirst at the water fountain in the main building, pretending to be deers in the forest as we wait silently for the rest of the class. "Ven acá," I gesture to Carlitos as we enter the classroom. I give him a sticker to place on the class chart for positive choices; the girls clap excitedly, exhorting the boys to follow directions so they can turn the kitchen into a restaurant after earning eight stickers in a row. I make a note to myself to have the children read the lunch menu in preparation for the event, as a perfect opportunity to model and practice word-attack skills for our more advanced readers.

As the children remove their coats, I ask all of you to meet me in front of the white board. By the time the last *chaqueta* has been hung to dry, I have taped a piece of butcher paper several feet long to its hard surface. Beto, Toño and their classmates take seats at my feet; I urge them to move closer to the board, requesting, "Ven acá, ven acá," with my words, wrists and hands. Uncapping a thick black marker, I ask everyone what we just did. A lively discussion breaks out among the group in both languages. After a time, I ask if our adventure in the blizzard was a story. After heartily agreeing, the enthusiastic group dictates the following text as I write in two inch thick letters for everyone to see:

> Today it is snowing. We went outside. We caught
> some snowflakes. Carlitos caught 5 snowflakes.
> Sergio caught 6 snowflakes. Patrick caught 9
> snowflakes. Arlene got 10. Toño caught 6 snowflakes
> altogether. John ate 19. Isabella ate 29 snowflakes.
> Beto ate more snowflakes than he could count.
> Then we came inside.

While reading and rereading our story aloud as it was being completed, I point and state each word aloud. The children read along with me, piping up at the sound of their names. I stop and sound out words, pretending they are rubber bands that can be stretched and associated with specific sounds. Individual students offer letters, sounds, and punctuation marks to the collective text.

When the narrative is finished, I ask if it is a *real story* with a beginning, middle, and an end. Beto walks to the front of the board, pointing out where the story starts while John authoritatively announces that I "didn't remember to write THE END" at the bottom of the page.

One by one, at my request, the children come to the chart to underline their names and circle specific letters, sight words, and numerals. We return to the story to read it one last time as a whole group. I ask Char if there is a part of a sentence or line she would like to read all by herself which she does quite easily. Eight hands shoot up into the air as I comment on how much I like to call on kindergarteners who I can tell are really thinking.

Once again, the children advance up to the chart to read individual words, phrases, and sentences. Jasmine proudly shares that she can read the entire story backwards. When the boys and Char protest, I turn to her and say, "Ven acá" with a knowing wink. Jasmine softly but defiantly calls out words backwards from any point of challenge in the text. The class is amazed. I assure them that they, too, will soon be able to accomplish the same feat if they keep listening to stories, learning their letters and words, and learning how to read and write. Later in the afternoon, I will type up the chart and create individual story books for each child to illustrate and read in whole, half, and small groups until they can read the work as individuals.

Sensing the kindergarteners need to move around, I quickly launch into a quick game, changing my tone to call out, "Simon says...stand up!" Those children who speak the language of the day immediately jump to their feet, pulling up their peers. I continue with, "Simon says...touch your head!" Nine pairs of hands rest quickly on their heads. Speaking a little faster, I challenge, "Simon says, write your name on top of your arm!" John and Charlene look around at their classmates to take up the cue. "Write your name under your foot!" I cry out. Jasmine starts to sit on the floor, then reverses her decision mid-flight. "Simon says, walk to the table, take out a pencil and place it on your seat." As the children transition to the next activity, I quickly mark down which students need more practice learning the parts of the body, school items, opposites, and academic commands.

During math, the kindergarteners do an excellent job of practicing basic addition and subtraction with poker chips, plastic math symbols, and table mats. When Charlene bumps John's mat, spilling it all over the floor, Toño laughs wickedly, causing him to cry even harder. Sergio leans over to John and says, "Ven acá, Juanito. Te ayudo," in a reassuring tone. Beto pats the boy on his shoulder. Toño stops laughing as I abruptly switch his name card to the red light.

"Sergio and Beto, thank you for reassuring John," I gush. Beto beams as I state, "That's exactly what friends do. You must be very popular." John nods as he sniffles tear tracks running down his nose.

All at once, Carlitos notices the design on the manipulatives looks like snowflakes. Knowing that he needs additional work on associating numerals with specific quantities, I ask him if he would be interested in making snowflake stories with me later during self-selection time. Toño cleans up everyone's chips without being asked, so I move his name back to the yellow lens on the stop light.

In keeping with our theme and language of the day, we conduct a read-aloud using Eric Carle's *Very Quiet Cricket*. During the reading, the children begin to argue whether this book is as good as the other six texts we have read for our author's study. I suggest that we wait until the end and ask Char to quickly grab a small piece of paper to take a vote. We'll use the data in a chart later during the week to practice counting our numbers.

"What was that?" asks Sergio. The kindergarteners are transfixed upon hearing a cricket sound at the end of the book. I look from side to side, pretending to be surprised. I wink at the children and suggest that if they are really quiet, the cricket in the book might sing again. The class urges me to read the last three pages for a second time. Beto's face is full of wonder as we arrive at the last page and a gentle rhythm churrs again. Toño jumps up, pointing to the little sound chip just inside the binding activated by turning the page. The class has a good laugh as we try it a third time. I place the text on top of the book case for the children to read on their own. Tomorrow, Beto will sit mesmerized, opening the toy book again and again.

Are you feeling a bit antsy? Me, too. I ask Jasmine to continue leading our game of Simon Says with Carlito's assistance. This request places the children in a cooperative exchange where they depend on each other's linguistic expertise in their native and emerging languages. We wave to Grandma Mela who heads out the door with papers for tomorrow's phonics lesson. Ms. Garcia, the reading specialist, will visit our classroom to present a mystery object, its letter and corresponding sound, and a catchy rap the children will sing, associating the sound with the letter. We have already used the same tune for a bouncing ball, clicking camera, and Leo the Lion. As we advance further into the alphabet, each session incorporates a short craft related to the featured letter sound.

I ask Sergio to announce that it is time for reading group. When John appears momentarily confused, Jazzy takes him by the hand. "Ven acá," she practices, walking him over to the bookcases where everyone is settling into a small circle. As I pass out multiple copies of Pat Mora's Oye al desierto/Listen to the Desert, the children remind me how they will behave during guided reading sessions when they are first and second graders. As soon as their responses convince us that they know what is expected of them, I wonder out loud if all the kindergarteners will make first grade choices in reading group today. John kindly suggests that Toño's name card could be moved back to the green lens if he follows directions. Indeed, the little boy is aware that his amiguito is one step away from loosing self-selection time. We heartily agree as a class that this is a wonderful option for Toño, complimenting John on helping his friends to make positive behavior choices. "Because that's what friends do," emphasizes Charlene.

Turning to the text, I cheer silently to myself, scanning the book-handling behaviors of our little group. Jasmine immediately opens the text to her favorite part while Beto visibly checks to see if the picture and letters on the front cover are right side up. In our previous sessions, he had not known how to open the exact same book properly. As we move through the lesson reviewing the name of the author, illustrator, beginning, middle and end of the book, I take mental notes, monitoring who needs more support with page turning, reading left to right, tracking words and sentences with el dedo magico or the magic finger. Our third pass through the work, the children have become familiar with the author's description of the desert climate, animals, and the overall plot of the book in both Spanish and English on alternative days. Toño calls attention to the fact that, pressed for time, I have skipped reading the dedication. We return to the start of the book for him to call out the words he remembers. They are not exactly correct, but I warmly praise his approximation with my voice, face, and hands noting, "That's very close to Ms. Mora's dedication! You remembered well!" Toño proudly announces that he will dedicate the next book he composes in writer's workshop to his sister, Marisol.

Testing the children's knowledge of numbers, I ask everyone to navigate to the specific page where the story begins. Because we have previously conducted a picture walk, offered predictions about the story line, and discussed distinguishing features of the desert animals presented in the work, today's lesson focuses our class on the aural and visual experience of syntax. We engage in an echo reading event where I model fluency with finger-to-eye correspondence, articulating meaningful bits of sentence architecture. The children echo my exact words, mimicking verbal gestures including emotional expression, emphases, and punctuation signals.

John jubilantly points to each word one at a time out of sequence, but his verbal responses follow in sync exactly with his *compañeros*. Sergio's finger moves smoothly from left to right; however, he has not yet matched the words he has memorized in his head with the print he anticipates on the page. Beto is not sure where to begin, so I ask Charlene to lean over and share the same book with him so he can see how she smoothly matches the written print and verbal text with her finger as a tool.

Toño politely suggests that we teach you to play the "question game" where the children pose inquiries for each other at the bottom of each page. Many of the kindergarteners have an advanced knowledge of the genre called "teacher talk," from playing school with older siblings, cousins, and *tíos*. I silently remind myself to hold a mini-lesson with the four kindergarteners in our tiny group whose decoding proficiencies have become sophisticated enough to diversify the types of questions they construct as a part of the meaning making process. Indeed, Char and Jazzy will engage in creating these very linguistic structures as they play "reading group" later during the morning self-selection time.

Our reading lesson concludes with a class cheer for Beto, who is able to point to the words "and" and "the" on several pages. The children take turns rereading their favorite part of the book, imitating the howl of a baby coyote in the desert. The call of the Southwest swells inside our little trailer. I reflect on the fact that most of the children's families and traditional cultures hold a sacred relationship to the animal, wondering how I might bring this perspective into our discussions next week.

Isabella compares her brand new watch to the one on the wall, announcing that it is self-selection time. Sighing, I inform the children we will write in our journals tomorrow, dismissing the children to choose one or two of a variety of activities with free access to drawing paper, stamps, cars, reading material and the class computer.

Personally, I will employ our last few precious moments of instructional time to help Sergio read the letter he has received from one of the secretaries from the main office; apply the rubber band method with Beto as a means of systematically recording the sounds in his last name; show the boys how to use a timer with large numbers on it to equitably share the most coveted matchbox car; and quiz Jasmine as to where she might include question marks and periods in a note she has written to her father. Our pre-lunch transition time will, no doubt, be accompanied by the multiple dramas associated with shifting from one authority figure to another.

But first, I search for Toño's hopeful face as his *amiguitos* race to their preferred activities in the classroom. "Ven acá," I wave to him smiling. We meet at the chart with the street light.

"What choices did you make during reading group?" I ask. The boy recants the positive actions he displayed in the little group. Nodding your head, you are very impressed. As Toño moves his name card from yellow to green lens of the stop light, a chorus emits from the plastic race track on the other side of the room, "Ven acá!"

CHAPTER FIVE

Tranformations in Emergent Biliteracy

By the end of May, both boys exhibited multiple strengths and integrated practices as readers, writers, speakers, and listeners in their first and second languages. Before delving into the nuts and bolts of their biliteracy development, let's examine why it is important for linguistically rich children to be at least partially educated in their native languages. Wouldn't more exposure to or use of English result in stronger L2 language and literacy proficiencies?

The Nature of Bilingualism and Biliteracy

The short answer is no. As monolingual Americans, we have harbored myths and misunderstandings regarding the nature of bilingualism. Research has established that, when it comes to bilingualism, less is never more and more is never less. Experts note that "proficiency in the home language does not have to result in reduced English language skills and, conversely, the development of English language skills does not have to entail the loss of the home language" (Genesee & Riches, 2006, p. 142). Indeed, we have incorrectly framed linguistically rich children as students with a "language barrier", challenged by the dichotomous mastery of two distinct codes. In truth, linguistic development is a much more sophisticated process than we ever imagined. We must redefine our notions of the linguistically rich child as an active, intelligent learner who draws on dual psycho-sociolinguistic systems by drawing on developmental interdependencies and parallel abilities between their multiple languages. Children like Beto and Toño need more than a "half education" in English. Like their English-speaking peers, they deserve a comprehensive, creative, and challenging curriculum that taps and nurtures their total academic potential.

Cognitive Advantages of Bilingualism and Biliteracy

Over 50% of the world's population speaks a second language; bilingualism is both a norm and necessity outside the United States. In addition to its many cultural, vocational, and economic benefits, bilingualism has been associated with a multitude of cognitive advantages. When compared to monolinguals, bilingual individuals exhibit superior competencies in divergent thinking, creativity, metalinguistic awareness, and communicative sensitivity, among other benefits (Baker, 2001). Scientists have concluded that the single greatest predictor of second language acquisition is the extent to which an individual's first language literacy (or L1 literacy) has been developed. Indeed, L1 literacy supports literacy in the second language. When we reframe our view of the linguistically rich child, it is not difficult to see why extensive schooling through the medium of two languages is superior to remedial instruction in one unfamiliar language.

Cross-Linguistic and Cross-Modal Relationships of the L1 and L2

Biliteracy involves a complex series of cross-linguistic and cross-modal relationships between a learner's L1 and L2 and oral and written proficiencies. In other words, when speaking, listening, reading and writing, intricate connections occur between and across a child's primary language of Spanish, Karen, or Lakota and English as an additional language. A host of parallel abilities or developmental interdependencies transfer across languages including background knowledge, conceptual knowledge, phonological awareness, letter knowledge, sound-symbol relationships, decoding skills, and comprehension strategies. Riches and Genesee (2006) observe that "aspects of both L1 and L2 oral proficiency are linked to L2 literacy development" (p. 72). For example, phonological awareness, or the knowledge that words are made of sounds, syllables, and rhymes, is a precursor to learning to decode print. In general, children who have strong phonological awareness more easily draw connections between sound and symbol relationships when learning to read. Researchers have found that once a child's phonological awareness is developed in their L1, the same ability can be applied cross-linguistically in the L2. Similarly, the various modes of speaking, listening, reading, and writing also reciprocally buttress and extend literacy proficiencies. For example, second- language learners with limited oral language can still develop phonological awareness in their L2 literacy by drawing on their knowledge in the L1.

Linguistically rich students draw on these language and literacy abilities regardless of the code in which they are reading or writing (Riches and

Genesee, 2006; Genesee and Riches, 2006). The developmental complementarities that exist between the L1 and L2 collectively inform, create, and enrich a "common underlying reservoir of literacy abilities" (Riches and Genesee, 2006, p. 77; Genesee, Lindholm-Leary, Saunders, and Christian, 2006). In fact, highly successful English language learners resource their L1 to decode, navigate, and make meaning with English text when reading. Jimenez (2000) discovered that highly competent biliterates were successful readers in both of their languages, while their less proficient peers struggled and employed different and less effective strategies when reading in both their L1 and L2 (Riches and Genesee, 2006). In short, effective biliterates develop an awareness of the relationships between their two languages and literacies. Reading is seen as a part of a larger process in which knowledge can be drawn from either language to support the goal of meaning making. This is why Lindholm-Leary and Borsato's (2006) studies of bilingual Hispanic children noted that these linguistically rich students "had higher achievement scores, G.P.A.s and educational expectations than their monolingual English-speaking Hispanic peers" (p. 203). When provided with sufficient time, instructional expertise, and sociocultural support, bilingualism and biliteracy are correlated with high academic performance in two languages.

Expert Support for Biliteracy

Unfortunately, many Americans remain unfamiliar with the scientific data that support the development of biliteracy for English-dominant and linguistically rich children. However, the National Literacy Panel (see August and Shanahan, 2006) widely considered the leading authority on reading and writing instruction, additionally concluded that teaching children to read in their L1 promotes reading achievement in their second languages. The panel, comprised of 18 experts in related disciplines, spent over 3 years combing over 3,000 international research reports on literacy development. After identifying 300 studies that met highly stringent scientific criteria, the group of scholars conducted a meta-analysis of 17 studies comparing reading instruction that employed children's first and second languages against instructional approaches that submersed the students in English (their L2) only. Goldenberg (2008), who served on the committee, observed the NLP "concluded that teaching English language learners to read in their first language and then in their second language, or in their first and second languages simultaneously (at different times during the day)...boosts reading achievement in the second language" (p. 14). The committee's statistical analyses suggested that elementary, secondary, and special education students who received two to three years of reading instruction in both languages, scored 12–15 points higher on reading tests than their contemporaries who received L2 literacy instruction alone. Goldenberg observed that these effects might have the potential to increase based on the length of time children receive bilingual instruction.

Goldenberg (2008) also cited the NLP report to be only one of five meta-analyses to establish the positive impact of L1 literacy on reading and writing in the L2. Researchers from the Center for Applied Linguistics (CAL) and Center for Research on Education, Diversity, and Excellence (CREDE) conducted their own meta-analyses, confirming the value and positive influence of linguistically rich children's L1 on their L2 oral language, literacy and educational achievement. Pre-school children who engaged in L1 literacy experiences in the home and school were found to progress more quickly and successfully when engaged in L2 literacy development than peers who were not exposed to L1 literacy (Genesee and Riches, 2006). Reese, et al. (2000) also established children's L1 reading proficiencies to be a significant predictor for L2 reading in English eight years later (p. 78 in Riches and Genesee, 2006). Similarly, Royer and Carlo (1991) noted fifth graders' ability to read in their L1 to be the best indicator of L2 literacy achievement in sixth grade (p. 78 in Riches and Genesee, 2006). Interestingly, L1 literacy was found to have a "more significant and positive developmental relationship with L2 literacy" than oral language proficiencies (Riches and Genesee, 2006, p. 69). These findings fall in line with multiple studies from the 1980s where immigrants who had acquired L1 language and literacy proficiencies within the formal educational systems of their home countries were more likely to achieve at the same level of native English-speaking students in English after moving to the United States (Lindholm-Leary and Borsato, 2006). In light of the data from studies on bilingual education models, second-language acquisition, and bilingual-biliteracy research, these results beg for the development of biliterate competencies as a serious educational alternative for linguistically rich students like Toño and Beto. Let's take a peek at what this process looked like for our two emergent biliterates between the months of December and May.

Beto's Emerging Proficiencies from December to May

Biliterate Foundations:
Aural Strengths, Oral Development, and One-Word Literacy

Aural strengths. Beto's auditory strengths provided the primary mode through which the young boy learned to navigate academic culture. While drawing and cutting were new to him at the start of the school year, Beto's superior listening proficiencies in Spanish far exceeded those of his peers in December. His capacity for visually reading the environment, aurally attending to others, and matching verbal and existential realities provided an underlying structure for his early school success. Our initial encounter indicated the child's strategic use of peer modeling and collaboration for linguistic, conceptual, and behavioral scaffolding: he dynamically observed his best friend select, cut, and paste pictures from a magazine before he was able to engage in the practice independently. Beto's active demonstration of courtesy, interest, and respect for the individuals with whom he interacted promoted his status as a student and friend in our small speech community. As the little boy slowly gained familiarity and trust in my expectations and speech patterns, Beto's ability to follow instructions in Spanish was expanded to include directives in English.

Oral development. In early September, school records indicated that Beto tested as a beginning English speaker on the Language Assessment Scale (LAS). The shy child exhibited symptoms of culture shock and did not speak in either Spanish or English for a long time. As a monolingual, Spanish-dominant student, he initially relied on imitating his peers' physical, emotional, and linguistic behaviors to forge new understandings between sign, meaning, and action. The first time I heard the intelligent child speak in English, Beto thoughtfully echoed one of his classmates. This instance of copycatting occurred the day Beto and Francisco included a new student in their play group during self-selection time. Patrick had reared the Tyrannosaurus Rex toy he was holding, shaking it vehemently at Beto's small plastic stegosaurus. In a low, booming voice, Patrick inquired threateningly, "Do you want a piece of me?!?"

The shy Beto immediately raised his smaller figure to the same height of the T-Rex. "Yeah!" he boldly challenged back. "I want a piece of you!"

Patrick pressed on challenging, "Then, come get me!" A brief silence ensued, followed by Francisco's rapid translations. Without missing a beat, a series of snarls and roars carried the communicative intent of the boys' exchange.

In my initial conversations with Beto, the little boy spoke quietly through his *amiguitos*. In fact, Beto did not independently address me in his home language until we had spent two and a half months together. After this time, the young child used Spanish almost exclusively to communicate with me from December through August. He continued to rely on friends and siblings to make his needs known in both languages. Among his peers, Beto's comprehension or listening phase (Krashen, 1981) in English extended until April when the child began to utter full sentences in play circles.

While Beto was silent approximately 97% of the time during this foundational period, gentle one-to-one encouragement allowed for the assessment of basic vocabulary in Spanish and English. In December, the good-natured boy counted from three to eleven and identified parts of the body in Spanish. Beto also employed a mix of codes to name the color words. He used Spanish terminology to label brown, purple, and green circles, and English vocabulary to distinguish yellow, blue, and black colors. When asked to identify a page of randomly assorted lowercase letters, the sweet boy erupted into the "ABC" song. Beto sang all the way to the letter "s" in English and then abruptly trailed off into silence.

Figure 1. Beto's Father.
Courtesy of the Artist and Family

While the smart child associated the song with the letters, Beto was just discovering that individual visual, kinesthetic, and written signs had the capacity to represent meaning. The development of this core understanding was necessary before the child was able to draw relationships between two random, abstract sign systems required for letter recognition and phonemic or letter-sound awareness. When asked to name the uppercase letters in Spanish or English in December, Beto verbally labeled the letters M, F, and S as "3," "5," and "1" in English respectively. The young boy was not yet able to distinguish between alphabetic and numerical symbols. During this interval, the child was also unsure which direction to hold or open a book even when the front cover sported the picture of an animal in which he was interested. The need to forge foundational concepts about signs was also reflected in Beto's writing from this period. The young boy preferred to watch his age mates draw instead of coloring himself. The one drawing Beto independently produced during this interval involved the basic application of circles and squares to depict his father (Figure 1). While the figure's simplistic features, block torso, and square legs are slightly reminiscent of the classic guppy figure, Beto accurately portrayed Eduardo's height and stance from the perspective of a small boy. Beyond this token symbol, Beto would not express the internalization and production of other individual signs until mid-spring.

One-word literacy. Beto's signature from this phase also suggested the development of foundational understandings between symbols and his lived experience. An initial assessment in December indicated the small boy was acquiring the fine motor control necessary for the construction of letters and numbers. During this period, Beto observed his age mates practice handwriting strokes, letter formations, and their signatures a great deal. The child was at a decided disadvantage in that his third kindergarten teacher had renamed him without his family's consent, insisting the boy write the name Roberto instead of Umberto. In light of this outrageous deviance, Beto's subsequent determination and effort to correctly write his own name is to be applauded.

In tracing the development of his signature, Beto employed the correct letters in his first name by mid-January. While he could not identify the names or sounds of the letters in his name, the intelligent boy relied on a kinesthetic protocol to execute each separate letter. The evolution of his signature involved the inclusion and disappearance of both upper- and lowercase letters, the sequencing of written signs from right to left and then left to right, letter reversals, the isolation of component sign parts, and the omission of elemental features of letters. Interestingly, the little boy worked diligently to learn his full legal first and last name at the same time. In negotiating this field-text relationship, Beto acquired foundational knowledge of the concepts of print including directionality, spacing, and an understanding of letters, initials, and words. The smart child transitioned from drawing letters to writing his name in early March. The achievement of this one-word literacy served as both a foundational magnet and hinge for Beto's emergent biliteracy proficiencies in his next stage of development.

Beto's First Transformation: Tri-linear Trajectories

Beto's development of concepts of print continued into the first transformation of his biliteracy acquisition. During this period, his understanding of written signs grew toward an understanding of texts. Beto's compositional proficiencies also originated at this time. Like three roads charted to end at one common point, these separate trajectories would eventually chart Beto's evolving path to an integrated crossroad.

Concepts of print. Beto's advances in handwriting persisted well into the mid-spring. During his first transformation, he was able to copy letters that were modeled for him with mixed results. Toward the end of February, several tiny triumphs or microgenetic changes were noted. Beto independently formed an upper- and lowercase letter for the signs Bb, Cc, and Dd. He also produced sounds for all three letters and identified Cc and Bb by name. After I demonstrated how he and Francisco might keep track of who won their car races, Beto showed great facility for the use of tally marks. By the end of March, Beto's ability to correctly formulate the letters in his name was well established.

The little boy's oral vocabulary also expanded during this time. Beto could list the main parts of the body. He also recited rhymes and songs about the days of the week and other topics. At the end of this phase, Beto counted up to nineteen in both Spanish and English.

Book knowledge and handling skills. The child also demonstrated significant growth in his knowledge of written print, texts, and books. In mid-February, we began reading groups with bilingual picture books. On the first day, Beto held the text upside down and attempted to open the book at its spine. By the end of four weeks, the smart boy used pictures and letters on the front cover to appropriately position books before opening them. Beto also learned to point to the title of the text and the author or illustrator's names. When each child was invited to read about their favorite animal from a repetitive story, Beto approximated his speech to the print while guiding his "magic" or index finger from left to right. Smiling, he articulated predictable words from the page in Spanish, followed by a tiny howl where the storyline correctly indicated a coyote's call. From time to time, Beto still required cues to follow the texts we read and revisited in class. However, his book handling knowledge and skills advanced from the need for physical modeling and scaffolding to the use of more abstract, visual, or verbal cues. The child's emerging ability to picture read and issue predictions specific to the visual storyline affirmed Beto had crossed a threshold into the world of books and was quickly advancing down a functional trail.

Emergent writing. The third line of development evidenced in Beto's first biliteracy transformation involved the child's first attempts at written composition. Concerned by the absence of drawings and letters in his journal, I included myself in one of Beto and Francisco's play sessions in February. As I watched the two boys play cars, we chatted about their friendship. Beto grinned when I suggested we write a story about the two friends. Graciously suspending their game, the two boys dictated the following narrative:

> *Umberto es reyno. Francisco es su amigo.*
> *Los niños juegan Nintendo.*
> *Los niños veen televisión. Los niños comen galletas.*
> *El fin.*

After inscribing each sentence in Spanish a few words at a time, I proposed we also include an English translation of their story. The boys heartily agreed, supplying me with the words they knew sentence by sentence. Their English version read as follows:

> Umberto is king. Francisco is his friend.
> The boys play Nintendo.
> The boys watch television. The boys eat cookies.
> The End.

The children concluded the writing session by agreeing to title the work, *Los dos amigos* or *The Two Friends*.

Several features of this text were significant for Beto. The narrative was the first story the child ever composed that was recorded on paper. Second, the story incorporated Beto's name and life experience as opposed to a fictitious character or animal. Third, the vocabulary reflected the little boy's oral proficiencies in his first and second languages. Both the syntax and genre of the writing resonated with the predictable big books we read together in class.

The next day, I presented each boy with a typed copy of the narrative in book form. We agreed their evening homework would be to illustrate the five pages of the text. We carefully read and reread each sentence of the book over and over again, discussing what the boys might draw on each page. The children practiced reading the predictable text to me and each other. Our joint practice, coupled by the significant features of text outlined above, fused the story in Beto's memory.

Ramón es reyno.

Ramón is a king.

1.

Figure 2. Beto's Self Portrait as King.
Courtesy of the Artist and Family

Two days later, Beto submitted an illustrated version of his book. The assignment required an extra day to secure his older sister's assistance. Like the drawing of his father, Beto created one individual sign for the narrative. His kingly self-portrait (see Figure 2) consisted of an amoeba-like body with four protrusions for arms and legs. The character's torso was topped by a circle head with circle eyes and a curved line indicating a mouth. The figure was crowned with a zigzag square. Multiple erasures on the page indicated Beto had made several suggested modifications under Tere or Miranda's guidance.

Beto applied his newly acquired book handling skills when he presented his story to the rest of the class. The work served as a catalyst, assembling the child's emerging proficiencies in concepts of print, book knowledge, and composition: *Los dos amigos* served as a prototype for several books to come.

Beto's Second Transformation: Holistic Emergent Biliteracy Processes

Beto's second transformation in emergent biliteracy acquisition occurred between mid–April and the end of school in late May. During this stage, the little boy's growth in concepts of print, book knowledge and handling skills, and writing composition shifted from three qualitatively distinct trajectories to a unified, holistic, and integrated process of emergent biliteracy.

Speaking Proficiencies

Beto's silent period in English ended at this time. Instead of advancing through Krashen's (1981) second language oral production stages in sequential order, the little boy remained silent until he could communicate with his friends in full sentences. The first complete, self-constructed sentence in English that I heard Beto utter also involved a play object. After he and a classmate finished speaking about a car or toy at home, Beto stated a matter of factly, "I'll bring it tomorrow." His proper use of a contraction and indirect object indicated a sophisticated pattern of syntax. During this transformation, Beto sometimes did not distinguish between the languages he used with monolingual speakers. For example, one morning in mid-April, Beto turned to an English-dominant classmate and commented, "Play with me. *Sergio no se habla inglés, pero yo sí.*" Beto did not realize he had switched codes mid-sentence to note Sergio's Spanish monolingualism and his willingness to translate. His classmate replied, "Let's play something else, Beto." The bilingual boy responded, "Okay, let's play another game." Beto then turned to Sergio to translate the exchange in Spanish.

A continuation of the same conversation highlighted Beto's integration of academic vocabulary into his verbal repertoire. As Beto, Bobby and Sergio created designs with rubber bands on geo-boards, Bobby inquired in English, "What are you making, Beto?" The little boy replied, "A triangle." Beto then translated the conversation to Sergio in Spanish employing the term *triangulo*. By the end of kindergarten, Beto served as a bilingual mediator between his classmates. He could verbally identify the basic colors and body parts in English and Spanish. The linguistically rich child counted from one to fourteen in Spanish and one to twenty in English, with the exception of omitting the transitional number of fifteen. He was also able to retell a simple picture story in chronological order using either language.

In light of Beto's full-sentence utterances, it is interesting to note that he did not independently choose to speak with me in English unless required in a testing context. Despite my intermediate proficiency in oral Spanish, he apparently did not regard me as an English-dominant speaker. Beto's aural proficiencies served him well on the days English was our language of instruction. At the end of May, Beto memorized and related his street address in English and Spanish. He sang four of our letter chants to himself in English when engaged in an independent activity.

Emergent reading. In late April, Beto continued to distinguish between numbers and letter signs. While the child counted up to fifteen in both languages, Beto needed support to develop the connection between numerals and their quantities. The forge between symbol and meaning was also absent in Beto's recognition of letter names. As the bilingual boy learned the ABC song in both Spanish and English, he identified the letters B and O by their names in Spanish for the very first time in April. The date of this accomplishment is significant considering the child had been writing the two letters as a part of his name since the start of the school year in September.

This development coincided with Beto's first indication of phonemic awareness. Because the majority of Spanish consonants retain the same sound as their English counterparts, we especially concentrated on his acquisition of the grapho-phonetic signs in his name and the first five letters of the alphabet during our independent work together. In mid-April, Beto correctly produced the /f/ sound for its corresponding letter. Ten days later, he identified the sounds for four more letters. By mid-May, the young boy was able to confirm the names of ten letters in English and Spanish, match their upper- and lowercase pairs, and orally produce the sounds for six written signs. This dramatic shift was precipitated by an essential discernment: For the first time,

Beto understood letters represented the sounds of speech *and* the sounds of speech communicated his lived experience.

Meaningless marks on paper transformed in Beto's eyes as the world of print assumed meaning for the young boy. At the very end of the school year, I observed Beto reading independently for the first time. The child sat on the floor with a copy of the book *Go Dog Go!* obscuring his face. We had read the story a few weeks prior. Beto held the text right side up, turning its pages from right to left, one at a time. Behind the cover, his warm brown eyes momentarily stopped to consider each picture and its subsequent lines of text. Beto whispered his version of the plot to himself, using the illustrations as cues. From time to time, he unconsciously pointed to a letter he recognized, silently mouthing its name or sound.

Emergent writing. Beto's new-found knowledge that letters represented speech sounds proved to be endemic of a larger understanding of signs in general. During the second transformation in the child's emergent biliteracy development, Beto exhibited a greater interest and enthusiasm for the writing process. After the success of "*Los dos amigos*," I revisited Beto's playgroup to initiate a second narrative. Beto and Francisco were playing with a miniature corral and plastic horses. Following the same protocol we previously employed, the boys dictated the following story:

Los caballos
por Umberto y Francisco
Los caballos viven en corral. El rancho está de México.
Los caballos comen hierba y pastura. Los caballos corren en la carretera grande.
Los caballos corren y ganan muchos premios.
Lluego, los caballos comen pastura y beben agua.
El fin

For the second time, the boys agreed to collaboratively compose an English translation for the narrative that read:

The Horses
by Umberto & Francisco
The horses live in the corral. The ranch is in Mexico.
The horses eat hay and grass. The horses run the long racetrack.
The horses run and win many prizes.
Afterwards, the horses eat hay and drink water.
The End

The next day, we reread the typed manuscript several times together. This time, the boys and I divided up the pages, brainstorming what pictures might illustrate each page. Just before lunch, Beto approached me with a worried look. The little boy explained he didn't know how to draw a horse. On a scrap piece of paper, I modeled how to depict the animal using the names of shapes we learned in math: A rectangle served as the horse's torso, propped up by four narrow legs of the same shape. An angled line supported a triangle head with a rounded point to represent the soft muzzle. Wavy lines constructed the perfect mane and tail, with a final circle for an eye. The eager child practiced the visual sign until he could draw the horse on his own. Greatly relieved, Beto tucked the scrap paper into his backpack just in time for the bell.

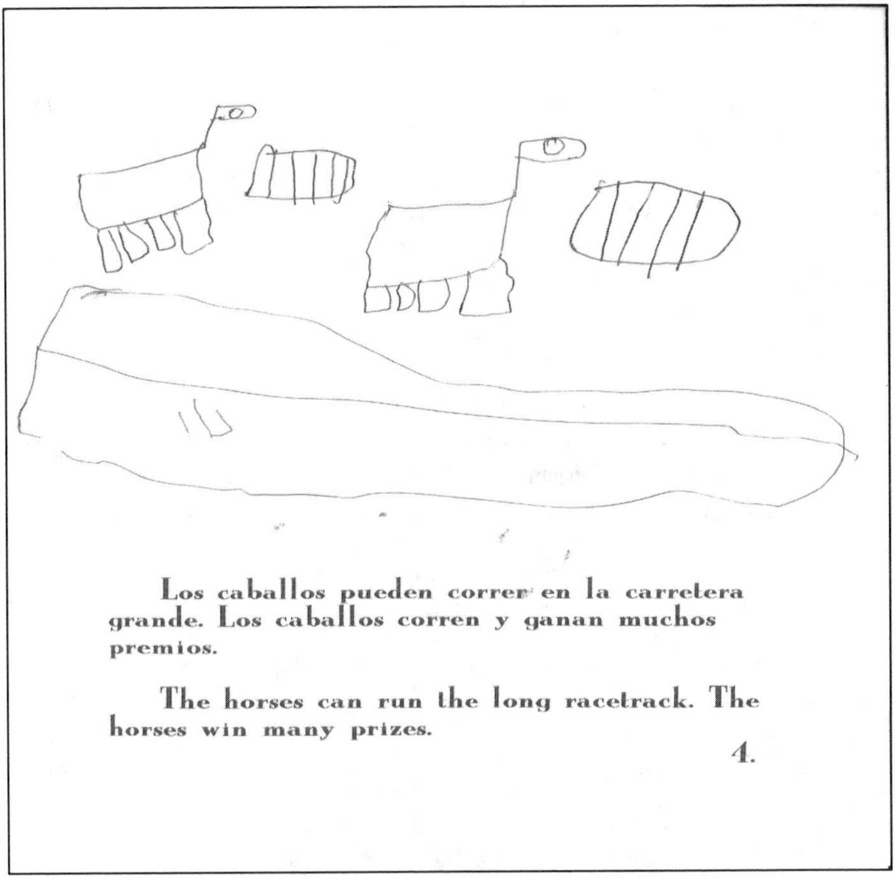

Los caballos pueden correr en la carretera grande. Los caballos corren y ganan muchos premios.

The horses can run the long racetrack. The horses win many prizes.

4.

Figure 3. Beto's Horses.
Courtesy of the Artist and His Family.

The next day, Beto sported a beaming smile as he submitted his homework. He illustrated one of the two assigned pages all by himself (see

Figure 3). On the fourth page of the book, the little boy depicted a long, oblong field with a line drawn through it to symbolize a racetrack. Two horses stand at separate rectangle gates waiting for a race to begin. Beto successfully symbolized his thoughts using the visual sign we practiced together. We were both proud he had accomplished such an important task independently without the assistance of his older sisters.

Figure 4. Beto's First Letter.
Courtesy of the Artist and His Family.

After the publication of The Horses/Los caballos in mid-April, Beto frequently asked me to show him how to draw signs for objects and animals. In early May, the smart child giggled with glee as I demonstrated how to draw a centipede out of circles and lines, placing a pair of eyeglasses over its nose. The next day, Beto gifted me with his first letter (see Figure 4). At the top of the page, the young boy had dictated the following message written by a family member: Este es para ti maestra te quiero. (This is for you teacher, I love you.) In the center of the page, Beto depicted our familiar worm floating above a horse. The equine was drawn in the same manner from our session two weeks ago. While Beto refined his placement of the worm's legs, the creature's circle eyes, button nose, and rounded antenna suggest a greater sophistication and attention to detail on the part of the young artist than previously evidenced.

Most importantly, the marriage between symbol and meaning was clear in visual form.

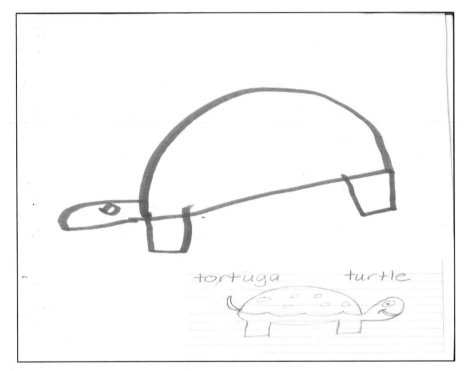

Figure 5. Beto's Turtle.
Courtesy of the Artist and His Family

Shortly after the worm was added to Beto's visual vocabulary, the little boy approached me and asked how to draw a turtle (see Figure 5). Out of the handful of signs we explored together, this symbol proved to be the most significant. The turtle appeared as a motif in the majority of literacy artifacts Beto interacted with or produced after that period: For the first time, Beto actually sought out others to dictate sentences and stories about turtles and requested books and magazines about turtles from the library. Blue turtles marched across Beto's journals for the remainder of the school year. The sign of the turtle proved to be the affective hook that snagged the little boy into the symbolic world of biliteracy, providing meaning and impetus for multiple reading and writing events in the summer months to come.

Tono's Emerging Proficiencies from December to May

Listening proficiencies. At first assessment in December, Toño did not appear to be much of an auditory processor. His vibrant, verbose personality seemed to override opportunities to listen to others in English and Spanish. Toño responded to verbal commands and storybooks in both languages when such directives or content interested him. Initially, the child appeared to have difficulty listening to other points of view or any discourse for an extended period of time. A month of careful observation passed before I figured out the intelligent child had mastered a well-rehearsed set of self-serving, pragmatic behaviors. Toño exercised a very deliberate, selective attention. While there were times he genuinely did not hear instructions, in many instances, Toño intentionally placed my adult requests into linguistic extinction. The day I first called his bluff, the little boy laughed good naturedly and sincerely complied with my direction. The game was over and I won his respect. From that point on, the sophisticated listener selectively added me to the list of interlocutors deemed significant in his world.

In December, Toño's independent, receptive abilities in English were very strong. The child comprehended the majority of most conversations and asked for clarity when he did not understand. Interestingly, Toño did not initially draw a connection between the Spanish used in his grandparent's home and that of the school. The first time I read a story in Spanish, Toño placed his hands over his ears. When I asked him why he covered his ears, the child replied that he didn't like it when I talked funny.

In reflecting on a conversation with his mother, I asked Toño if he ever spoke with his grandpa or grandma. After the little boy nodded and laughed, I asked him *in Spanish* if he understood when his grandparents spoke with him. The child again nodded and laughed at my ridiculousness. I then informed Toño *in English* that I had just spoken in Spanish similar to his grandparents. A look of surprise covered Toño's impish face. I explained that his family spoke in two ways, employing the languages of English and Spanish, and that we'd also be using both means of communication at school. We talked about how Toño could listen for words his *papi* and *abuela* used and how they might sound different than the words his parents spoke. This interaction signaled the start of Toño's growing sensitivity to the bilingualism in his environment. Unlike many children from bilingual homes, I do not believe that he actually understood that his family utilized two distinct codes. He never exhibited any disrespectful or negative behaviors toward Spanish use again.

During self-selection time, the little boy played by himself 60-70 % percent of the time. It is interesting to note that the remainder of this English-dominant speaker's free play was engaged with his monolingual Spanish-dominant peers. It was not unusual to observe Toño engaging in self-talk in English while his *amiguitos* spoke exclusively in Spanish while playing cars. As Toño's age mates slowly entered his solitary play circle, the little boy's desire for friendship necessitated the development of attentive listening, turn-taking, positive attention, and sensitive responses.

Toño's receptive proficiencies were additionally applied as the child became familiar with school routines, commands, and protocols in both languages. Often the creative boy sang songs to himself, emphasizing complicated consonant complications from the chants we had sung once or twice together. By May, Toño responded to verbal commands, language games, and storybooks equally in Spanish and English.

Speaking proficiencies. Toño's speaking proficiencies in December also reflected strong foundational processes for biliteracy. A highly verbal, non-stop, English-dominant speaker, Toño displayed an increased awareness of the sound patterns he produced. Given sufficient attention and appealing subject matter, Toño dominated peer and adult conversation partners for extended periods of time. When he wasn't talking to the individuals in his environment or the cartoon characters he watched on his home television with glee, the little boy engaged in a great deal of cryptic self-talk in English. Toño's incidence of egocentric speech and controlling discourse tended to diminish during periods of improved attendance. In the late spring, the wiry child was able to patiently collaborate in small group discussions involving rhymes, chants, shared writing, and choral reading.

Toño's full-volume, screaming tantrums provided an early indicator of his sophistication in using language as a tool. These fits included rageful yelling, crying, wailing, table–pounding, and persistent arguing over power issues. As soon as the child knew he had won a battle, Toño exhibited an instant change in self-comportment characterized by tremendous self-control. On a few occasions, I observed Toño physically assault his parents when whining, yelling, or fighting did not effect circumstances in his favor. With the exception of one regressive episode in May, hitting and kicking were not included in his repertoire of tantrum behaviors with me.

Toño's first major tantrum in our classroom occurred in mid-December when he preferred to continue playing with a favorite toy when it was time to go to lunch. Instead of attempting to control, silence, or give in to his behavior, I discovered Toño responded to the use of play therapy techniques presented by Axline (1967). Sitting on the floor to equalize our physical size difference, I repeated or echoed major portions of the child's sentences in a soft, soothing, neutral tone. Eventually, this practice diffused Toño's emotional state to a place where he was able to sit beside me so we might talk to each other. This protocol became a routine when the child began to exhibit tantrum behaviors. By early February, Toño's outbursts decreased sharply.

These de-escalating sessions are especially important to note for four reasons. First, it was during such interactions that Toño initially lowered his affective filter (Krashen, 1981) or psychic shield to a state where I could reassure him of my care. Second, the resulting talks allowed me to inform and shape his choices to better meet the social conventions of the situation. Toño's classmates responded to his tantrums with anger, terror, and annoyed indifference, jeopardizing his status in our small speech community. Third, our conversations provided an opportunity to appropriately advocate and negotiate for his needs using language in a novel and effective manner. In these zones of proximal development, Toño began to develop the interpersonal patience, turn-taking practices, and temporary suspension of certainty required for the development of two languages (Vygotsky, 1978).

With time and trust, Toño's tantrums were significantly reduced to be replaced by more socially approved speech conventions. We negotiated between the child's need to be heard and his position within the class as a larger speech community. Toño's desire to forge and maintain friendships in class motivated a more conscious, mindful manner of voicing his concerns, needs, or desires. Toño was slowly acquiring the pragmatic use and expressive power of language for Spanish and English.

In December, Toño did not initially exhibit productive Spanish proficiencies, although he may have possessed the ability to converse in a limited fashion. However, the child's oral phonology reflected a combination of Spanish and English sounds. To a lesser degree, this same duality characterized the energetic child's syntactical system. At times, the structure of Toño's sentences sounded like "baby talk." He would often eliminate pronouns and articles, using negation, possession, and verb tense in a developmental manner. In the early winter months, it was not uncommon to hear Toño formulate statements, questions, or negations using a hybrid of English-Spanish syntax. When Toño's cumulative records arrived from Santa Ana Elementary in March, I noted that a Language Assessment Scale (LAS) had not been administered to determine either the child's English or Spanish proficiency. While the test has questionable value in its alleged assessment of kindergarteners' second-language proficiencies, results from the oral component of the evaluation might have identified additional academic support services for the little boy.

The testing staff at Mariposa Elementary attended to the test administration immediately. It is significant the evaluation sampled Toño's basic interpersonal communication skills (Cummins, 1981) and knowledge of school objects on a test designed for children acquiring English as a second language. Despite the fact that Toño's parents had interacted with him in English during the majority of his formative years, the child scored mid-range on a scale from zero to five in English. The tester expressed concerns regarding Toño's oral syntax or verbal ability to construct sentences and questions following the conventional rules of English. Due to the late date and a shortage of trained speech therapists, Toño's referral was shelved until the following year. Toño's speech continued to be characterized both by developmental structures and English-Spanish hybridity across the summer months.

However, within a proactive and predictable educational context, Toño's aural and verbal proficiencies developed in a reciprocal manner. The little boy responded dramatically to play-based, child-centered, and direct instruction. In time, Toño felt safe asking questions when he was unsure of the meaning of directions or discourse. The smart child worked hard on raising his hand before interjecting his rapid-fire thoughts. A good-natured boy at heart, Toño often used English to direct, describe, or demonstrate concepts or conditions in his evolving friendships.

Because Toño was still developing vocabulary in English and Spanish, the little boy often did not articulate the proper label for an object, individual, or phenomenon. Toño employed one of two strategies when his communicative intent overshadowed his available lexicon. In the first approach, the little boy combined verbal, kinesthetic, and aural codes to express his thoughts. For example, in the late spring, one of Toño's peers wished to draw a picture of a motorboat in his journal. As his *amiguito* waited for me to finish with another child, Toño glanced at his friend's paper. He exclaimed, "That's right! You need a *chum*! *Chum*! *Chum*! *Chum*!" The tiny boy leaned over and moved his right hand and arm in a diagonal line backwards from below his knee to just above his neck four times. Then drawing a box with his hands, Toño stood upright, waved his ten fingers, and produced a loud buzzing noise. He continued the charade of acting out a high-powered boat engine by extending his right hand as though it was an arrow, and running across the room in the same direction.

The second strategy Toño employed involved the invention of novel, descriptive verbal categories capturing the qualities or functions of the object, individual, or phenomenon he wished to articulate. For example, when Toño was considering the creation of a mobile later during the summer, he gestured toward a hanger lying on the supply table. He requested that I pass the "carpet spanker." While he could not recall or did not know the proper term for a hanger, in this instance, Toño's careful observations of his grandmother's housecleaning practices provided the basis for his generative lexicon. Such creative proficiencies proved necessary to the boy's evolving linguistic system as a means of supporting his intra-personal or self-to-self meaning-making processes in light of his developing syntax and vocabulary.

The growth of Toño's English-Spanish bilingualism in school can be attributed to his attitudinal shift toward his Spanish-speaking teacher and peers. While his punctuality and attendance remained a prohibitive factor, by the end of May, the child immersed himself joyfully in most classroom activities on the days he attended school. Toño's classmates responded to positive changes in his temperament and behavior and eventually invited him into their cooperative work and play sessions.

By the time school dismissed for the summer, Toño's receptive and productive proficiencies in academic Spanish had increased. He could understand, follow, and execute school commands in Spanish. Toño actively sought out his Spanish-dominant friends during free play sessions. The energetic boy attended during Spanish read-alouds, often eliciting comments in English that appropriately corresponded to the story line in Spanish. Toño often echoed Spanish words under his breath and engaged in play talk using Spanish phonology. While his oral production in Spanish was limited to one- or two-word sentences and the deliberate utterance of common swear words, Toño's progression from Krashen's (1981) comprehension phase to the stage of early speech proved highly significant. By the start of the study, Toño's oral and verbal proficiencies in English and Spanish firmly rooted his road to biliteracy.

Emergent reading. In December, several of Toño's proficiencies as an emergent reader were well established due to the many hours of reading his aunt and sister had spent engaging the little boy. Our initial encounter revealed an extensive amount of text knowledge and book handling practices. Toño knew how to hold books and magazines right side up, to open texts from left to right, and to read the pages in order one at a time. Occasionally, the active child skipped a page or three or four in his haste to view colorful graphics of interest.

Toño also began kindergarten as an avid picture reader. He understood certain books told stories like the cartoons he watched at home, while other texts related information like his animal shows. He approached narrative and expository texts using two different speeds. When an interesting insect or reptile leapt from the pages he surveyed, the curious thinker slowed down to study the creature's unique anatomical details. It was not unusual for Toño to picture-read three to four texts in one fifteen-minute setting. In December, Toño was well aware that curious objects, beautiful places, and hilarious characters he would often animatedly speak to lay in the worlds between the pages of a book.

Toño's interactions with visual text revealed an emerging proficiency to make meaning with the indices, icons, and whole words located in his environment. He understood print represented speech and thought in both English and Spanish. Toño was especially sensitive to the coded symbols older members of his family valued and employed to negotiate their lives. For example, the little boy identified McDonald's golden arches as the restaurant his older brother preferred for French fries over other fast food chains. On the days he stayed home from school, Toño watched a great deal of television. Extensive electronic stimuli functioned as a broad resource for symbols, imagery, and world knowledge from which Toño bridged his virtual experiences and material realities. In early winter, Toño knew there was a difference between numbers and letters although he could not distinguish between the two symbols. Toño's visual memory galloped away with his mind. As an emergent reader, he was ready to pop.

In December, Toño was able to identify the names of eight letters of the alphabet in English. Toño's report card from early spring noted he recognized fifteen upper and lowercase letters. By the end of May, the child could name thirty-three out of fifty-two letters of the alphabet in English. Further, he matched sixteen upper- and lowercase pairs and produced sounds for the same signs. Toño's letter and sound recognition of the Spanish alphabet lagged behind his dominant language. He was able to articulate the phonemic equivalents for a handful of consonants in his heritage language. With so many absences, the integration of Toño's vivid imagination, alphabetic principle, and story knowledge provided a strong foundation for early, independent reading in English.

By the end of the school year, he applied picture cues to predict words and logical outcomes for the books he individually and collectively read. His story retellings revealed a balanced sensitivity to basic narrative structure and essential plot details. Toño loved to read his name in the stories we composed as a class on chart paper. His peers displayed a host of emergent reading behaviors. By attending only two or three days a week, Toño's opportunities to model and participate in reading events remained restricted. While the child would engage in private speech with the subjects of the texts he interacted with, outside of picture and symbol reading, he did not show any interest in decoding print. The emergent biliterate, however, backed into reading through the writing process.

Emergent reading. The transformations evidenced in Toño's writing reflected his dramatic evolution as an emergent biliterate. The little boy's handwriting, signature, sign formation, and compositional proficiencies independently and interdependently developed across four phases. Three stages averaged a nesting period of approximately thirty days after which the internalization of novel practices was complete. Revolutions in Toño's writing development were characterized by instances of reversal or recycling where previously established proficiencies resurfaced like the structures of an underwater kingdom revealed at low tide.

Foundational writing proficiencies. A handwriting exercise from early December indicated Toño was well on his way to mastering the foundational strokes necessary to formulate letters and numbers. An oversized, unlined page of lines, circles, and curves confirmed the child's large motor control, while spiraling edges and open spheres revealed the continuing development of fine manual dexterity.

Figure 6. Toño's First Family Portrait.
Courtesy of the Artist and His Family.

In December, the intelligent child was able to formulate all the letters in his first name. While he could not identify the names and sounds of more than two letters, Toño had memorized a kinesthetic procedure allowing him to sign in each day and label his papers. With the exception of one letter, he represented his name using uppercase letters exclusively and only reversed one sign. Initially, the young boy inscribed the letters of his name from right to left and bottom to top, employing the right edge of the paper as a visual and physical anchor.

Toño's drawings from this foundational phase depended on line to symbolize his subject matter. In an early family portrait (see Figure 6), Toño labeled his name on the right side of the document using the same protocol described above. On the left side of the paper, Toño recorded five stick figures in descending order. Visual signs created from circle heads and stick torsos symbolized the boy and his mother, father, sister, and brother. A fluid, dense line was employed to indicate hair, eyes, and curved mouths.

The majority of the visual subject matter presented a drawing of Toño's parent's rental house. In contrast to his stick figures, the building was constructed from closed shapes captured using a contour line. In the drawing, a sidewalk leads past a car to a house with a handled door, windows, and benches. Areas of the yard where Toño and Sol played in the dirt are shaded by a short tree. The child represented a run-down automobile used for parts located in back of the house. Mountain vistas are depicted in the distance. While the portrait itself did not relate a story per se, the drawing was replete with details about the boy's life. In visiting the same scene six months after Toño executed the drawing, I was astonished to witness the elements of the drawing in the exact placement of Toño's graphics.

Toño's First Transformation: Multimodal Meaning Making

The first transformation in Toño's writing development was characterized by multimodal meaning making during the composition process. For example, when drawing in his journal, Toño danced, spoke, sang, and acted out his ideas as he set visual signs down in color. Drawing was not only a natural extension of his speech and motion (Mahn, 1997), but a joyful means of self-initiation and direction. It was not unusual to witness Toño fluctuate between cryptic self-talk and social interaction when writing during this period.

The first indication of a qualitative transformation in Toño's writing proficiencies appeared in early January when the little boy wrote his nickname on our daily sign-in sheet. It was significant that the child inscribed "Toño" instead of "Antonio" for a few reasons. First, Toño's four previous teachers called him by his full name. Our class had adopted his family's term of endearment after spending our first week together. Second, I had not shown him how to write his alias. Third, the act of writing an abbreviated version of his full name indicated a break from the kinesthetic protocol Toño had previously relied on. The action required the syllabication of his first name, selection of a partial segment of the word, and the assignment of conventional phonemic knowledge to individual and collective abstract signs. Toño was breaking out of a kinesthetic, whole-word literacy into a writing system in which multiple visual components forged symbolic relationships to each other. During this period, the intelligent boy also began to print his name from left to right. The occasional use of scribbles appeared in his journal following the acquisition of these directional conventions. Toño also made his first attempt at writing his last name during this phase, successfully depicting three out of five letters.

Figure 7. Toño's Second Family Portrait. Courtesy of the
Artist and His Family

Toño's drawings from this multimodal stage originated with gestural action, brief sketches, and cryptic self-talk in English. An additional self-portrait from the period, not shown here, indicated the transference of his dramatic motions from kinesthetic to verbal and visual signs. Like previous drawings, Toño originally used line to construct his body from a cross and a circle. However, the use of shape was employed in this drawing for the first time with squares and triangles extending the fullness of his character's arms, chest, torso, and legs. Circle eyes and a button nose confirmed the shift from broomstick figures to active human beings constructed from solid shapes. Toño also portrayed himself using his favorite color of green. Dancing clouds emerged from a sky of blue shapes including the small corona of a sun.

A second family portrait (Figure 7) from the same time span additionally reflects a greater sophistication of icons to represent people. In contrast to his drawing from December, all of Toño's family members are composed from contour shapes. With the exception of his sister's stick arms and hands, Toño's illustration reveals a greater complexity in visual memory, manual dexterity, and procedural knowledge. These advances in sign development allow for a more concise depiction of the personalities, roles, and relationships that comprise his family.

Figure 8. Toño's First Man-Eating Sea Creature Drawing.
Courtesy of the Artist and His Family

Themes of self, family, and relationship can be contrasted with a final piece of Toño's artwork from the multi-modal period. Whereas the little boy's previous drawings portrayed the people in Toño's life, the depiction of a shark-like creature (see Figure 8) contains elements of a narrative. Close inspection of this drawing reveals a large turquoise and yellow zig-zagged fish suspended mid-page. The sea monster peers out of a black pupil inside a green eye with a smile exposing sharp, red, bloody teeth. The small figure of a human protrudes from the mouth of the creature exhibiting a distinctive frown on its face. An arrow penetrates the back of the water beast denoting cause and effect. In questioning Toño about his writing, the little boy pointed to each visual image of his story in a sequential fashion, recounting a switch in roles as the diver unsuccessfully attempted to spear the sea creature. Toño integrated gesture and the use of index to compose and retell his narrative. The drawing represents Toño's first attempt at signifying a story line involving conflict and action.

Toño's Second Transformation: Confluence

Transformations in Toño's writing development from mid-February to mid-March involved the confluence or orchestration of emerging proficiencies. Oral, kinesthetic, visual, and written sign use converged to produce an explosion in sign development. Toño alternated between writing his full first name and nickname, occasionally using lowercase letters instead of uppercase forms. The little boy continued to acquire the spelling of his last name with equal success, reversing very few letters when all the signs were represented.

During this period, Toño completed homework sheets involving the practice of letter and number exercises. These tasks also included the identification of upper- and lowercase letters as matched pairs. While the little boy used less private speech, Toño delighted in the silly chants we sang that coordinated the letter names, their sounds, and the movements required for drawing each sign. On occasion, the little boy publicly broke out in song, outlining a specific motion or letter associated with the chant in the air. During a spot check of his knowledge of the letter sounds, the little boy reverted to our chants remarking "My brain sings the song to myself."

Transformations in Toño's journals included the appearance of hieroglyphic-looking figures resembling abstract skulls, beetles, and all-knowing eyes (see Figure 9). The block, contour shapes of previous imagery now incorporated complicated, internal details usually neglected by the everyday observer. The little boy also expressed an interest in maps, arriving late to school one day due to a cartographic exercise. On arrival, his mother exasperatedly explained that Toño had calmly, slowly, and deliberately recorded every turn in the path from the front door of his house to that of his classroom. The map he produced included a line for each city block accompanied by dots for the approximate number of steps or minutes required to cover each distance. This document denoted that Toño had imbued abstract sign elements with personal meaning to create a symbolic representation.

Figure 9. Toño's Hieroglyphic Journal Signs.
Courtesy of the Artist and His Family

Additional developments in the child's scribble writing indicated a transition from the solitary use of wavy, curved lines to a combination of lines and print-like formations (see Figure 10). These seminal signs were restricted to the first few letters of the alphabet, the numbers 1–8, and uppercase letters from Toño's first name. After the introduction of letter writing and a classroom post office in preparation for Valentine's Day, hearts, arrows, x's, stars, and dollars and cents signs appeared in his scripts.

Perhaps the most remarkable revolution that occurred during this phase involved Toño's creation of multiple genres of literary artifacts. For example, the creative boy produced a drawing that represented the front and back of an envelope when folded over (see Figure 11). On the front of the document, Toño illustrated a stamp, addressed the envelope using the consonants of the addressee's name, indicated the cost of delivery with a dollar sign, and incorporated a tiny, cryptic drawing of the location to which the envelope was intended to be delivered. On the back of the paper, Toño depicted the actual seams of an envelope. The missive inside contained three documents including a small drawing of the recipient and the author, a student-created valentine, and a hand-produced $1,000,000,000 bill. When quizzed regarding their significance, Toño noted these marks with the seriousness of a professional publisher.

Figure 11. Toño's Fold-Over Envelope.
Courtesy of the Artist and His Family

In terms of composition, Toño's narratives incorporated a confluence of visual and written signs within temporal schemes. The man-eating sea creature resurfaced as a visual motif with two significant additions (see Figure 12). A line of hieroglyphic text accompanied the drawing in a bubble over the monster's head. Toño supplemented his iconography with the use of line as an index, suggesting a beginning, middle, and end to the visual tale. In reading his writing to me, Toño's finger followed the line, indicating the first action where the shark noticed a lone swimmer out of the corner of his glassy eye. Moving his finger to reflect a secondary action, the beast then turned to capture his prey with a giant tongue. Toño's motions suggested the next line denoted that, as the monster resumed his silent, predatory path, the brutal beast chomped down on his helpless victim. This visual horror story reflects a rich and sophisticated plot, summarized with a sweep of Toño's small fingers across the top of his hieroglyphic statement.

Figure 12. Toño's Second Man-Eating Sea Creature Drawing.
Courtesy of the Artist and His Family

In another picture-narrative about mummy treasure (see Figure 13), Toño first printed his name on the paper and then proceeded to draw a combination of pictures and written text before asking to dictate a story. His request was significant, being the first time the little boy sought adult assistance to record the words to a narrative. In reading his drawing, Toño depicted two stick figures engaged in separate actions. A figure on the right side of the drawing stands with raised arms above an inscription below his feet. The stick figure on the left side of the page is involved in another activity altogether. Toño noted with his fingers that an arrow indicated the two figures moved from the space above to a lower location where a marked box awaited them. In dictating the story, Toño related the following words:

Figure 13. Toño's First Mummy Treasure Narrative.
Courtesy of the Artist and His Family

One day, Ramon and Sergio finding some treasure.
This is the mummy treasure.
They opened the treasure and it had toys and coins.
The End

Like the playful rehearsals of the young artist himself, Toño's characters crack the code on a mysterious map to discover buried treasure. It is noteworthy Toño used the names of two of his Spanish-dominant classmates to name his action heroes. In terms of composition, the content of the dictation and drawing correspond exactly. The narrative consists of a beginning and middle with interesting details as well as an end recorded in visual and written signs. The use of oral language specific to narratives signifies a shift in Toño's acquisition of academic language in English.

Toño's Third Transformation: Synchronicity

Toño's final metamorphosis as a writer during the academic year was characterized by a synchronicity of aural, kinesthetic, verbal, and written modes of sign use previously assembled in late winter. The integration of these proficiencies lasted approximately forty-one days from late March through late April.

At the start of this phase, the bright boy continued to encode from left to right while silently mouthing the syllables of his full first and last name. Toño's use of private speech was greatly reduced. Both his wavy scribble writing and hieroglyphics disappeared, replaced by strings of letters with long lines underneath them. These letter strings were composed from a wide variety of clearly recognizable, reversed, upper- and lowercase letters. The strings were additionally accompanied by a few numbers with their own distinct location on the page.

When asked to read his novel scripts, Toño had added another genre to his growing list of literary artifacts. The text of letter–strings proved to be the child's personal rendition of the supermarket advertisements we had been reading during math time. Pointing to the letter strings, Toño recounted descriptive sentences and the prices of products similar to the grocery announcements we had been using to identify foods and practice reading numbers. Indicatory lines from Toño's drawings were now employed as a mneumonic device to cue which letters were to be read as sentences. In touching each individual mark above the indice or "sentence marker," Toño's novel use of sign also involved the depiction of individual letters as representatives for distinct words.

After the initial emergence of the letter-string sentences, Toño's writing appeared to go through a recycling phase for an interval of eight days. He reverted back to the use of sketchy, gestural line drawings in his journal. His letter formations during this time were very loosely connected. Elemental components of lines, curves, and circles seemed to only haphazardly constitute alphabetic resemblance. Toño's drawings included a large amount of thick, side-to-side scribbling marked by tight cross hatches of random movement. I was concerned to observe what I considered careless, simplistic, and regressive work from a sophisticated writer.

Around this time, Toño gifted me a set of baseball cards he created from scrap paper at home (see Figure 14). Each card was labeled with a numeral from one to five in the right hand corner. At first impression, the center of each card seemed littered with a confusing jumble of lines, circles, and scribbled pencil marks. Closer examination revealed dense, highly complex sketches of baseball players in motion. The depiction of a batter, fielder, pitcher, catcher, and base player was all the more remarkable because Toño did not play baseball or collect baseball cards.

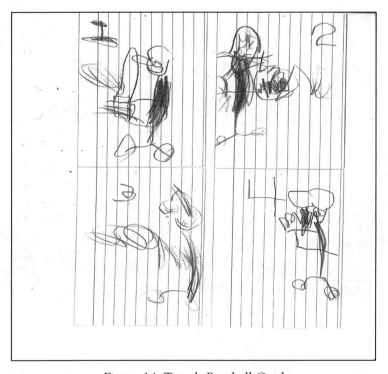

Figure 14. Toño's Baseball Cards.
Courtesy of the Artist and His Family

Eight days later, a transformation had occurred in Toño's writing. The complex, undulating lines of his drawings were mirrored in painstakingly shaped, intricate, lowercase letters. Where Toño previously insisted on working alone, he now delightfully related dictations in full sentences to whoever would write for him. Toño's compositions expanded to include jokes and other amusements that verbally played on poetic features such as onomatopoeia, alliteration, or assonance in English. The little boy read his journals to his peers, laughing as he related musical sentences including, "It is a sunny day for sun flowers." and "I like chicken and crumpled skin." In one of his last entries, Toño invented, dictated, and illustrated a "chicken cooking corn" as a new chant for the class to learn the letter "c." A nesting period of approximately six days was observed before any novel elements appeared in the child's writing.

Figure 15. Toño's Chinese Calligraphy.
Courtesy of the Artist and His Family

A final artifact evidenced Toño's emergence into biliteracy (see Figure 15). One day in late April, the elfish child nonchalantly handed me a paper with my name, Ms. C. written on it. After the child abruptly walked away, I noted a series of crossed slashes, random dots, and curved marks that I had never seen arranged in his writing before. Fearing the worst, I called Toño back to my side to get some insight into what I dreaded to be a back slide in his writing development.

"Read me your story," I urged him. I wanted to know exactly what was going on in his head at the time he constructed the drawing. Toño looked at me, frowned with displeasure, and attempted to leave the scene.

I implored the little boy, *"Mijo, ven acá."* (My dear son, come here.) Placing an arm around his waist to prevent escape, the two of us looked at the paper together. "Read me your story," I repeated.

Toño eyed me sideways in a cross manner and issued a rather pronounced sigh of boredom. Not to be dismissed, I persevered and gently requested, *"Mijo,* what does your story say?"

The little boy turned to face me with a look of impatient exasperation and snapped, "How should I know? It's in Chinese!"

Toño's invented script indeed mimicked the ideographic characters of Chinese. More importantly, like the Spanish he shared with his grandparents and *amiguitos,* a parallel had been drawn between the multiplicity of oral codes and their written signs. Toño had crossed the threshold into biliteracy. He carried these synchronized proficiencies into the summer months when the gentle summer winds blew across the Science Park in the Gallegos barrio.

Portraits in Meaning Making

Vygotsky and Meaning Making

Vygotsky offers us powerful conceptual tools to understand and appreciate Toño and Beto's development of listening, speaking, reading and writing proficiencies in Spanish and English as acts of meaning making. His ideas about the human mind differ from many schools of thought in two main ways. First, cultural-historical theory views the learner as an active, complex creator—a type of social architect, artist, or inventor. When we are engaged in the act of wondering, thinking, or learning, we are expanding our consciousness and lived experience through meaning making. Second, the relationships in which we are engaged are central to the social construction of meaning. As we interact with people, places, things, and ideas, we actively filter, organize, and attribute sense and significance in our lives through all of our senses. It is fascinating to consider that the human body allows for visual, aural, verbal, kinesthetic, tactile, and olfactory modes of meaning-making; these multimodalities correspond directly to the range of semiotic means we use to represent internal and external thought through art, music, dance, and language (Vygotsky, 1986; John-Steiner, 1995).

The Zone of Proximal Development

Vygotsky also offers us a novel way to define the substance of what we wonder, think, or learn about. Instead of seeing knowledge as a sterile, emotionless, disembodied assemblage of concepts independently suspended in the intellect, we can think of meaning as a cognitive-affective, multimodal tapestry of "culturally shaped understandings in which people organize their views of themselves, of others, and of the world in which they live" (Bruner, 1990, p. 139). Because these cultural meanings or semiotic texts differ across individual physiologies; psychologies; and social, historical, and political contexts, it is only reasonable to conclude that knowledge/cultural meanings will vary among human communities. As each of us are "assigned different activities and engage in different practices," we additionally construct our own "alternative resources and limitations for developing knowledge" (John-Steiner, 1999).

Meaning making occurs as the result of interactions taking place within two key contexts. The zone of proximal development (ZPD) is a psychological support existing between "the actual developmental level [of the learner] as determined by independent problem-solving and the level of potential development as determined through problem-solving under adult guidance or in collaboration with more capable peers" (Vygotsky, 1978, p. 86). A ZPD "awakens a variety of internal developmental processes that are able to operate only when the child is interacting with people in his environment and in cooperation with his peers" (Vygotsky, 1978, p. 90).

Perezhivanie or Lived Experience

Vygotsky's concept of the perezhivanie additionally explains the social nature of meaning making. This psychological phenomenon can be compared to a cognitive-affective prism through which "individuals perceive, experience, and process the emotional aspects" of a given circumstance (Mahn and John-Steiner, 2002, p. 49). Vygotsky (1994) described the perezhivanie as a dialectical experience occurring between the meaning-maker and her environment including "how a child becomes aware of, interprets, [and] emotionally relates to a certain event" (p. 341). The personal dimension of the perezhivanie encompasses the total sum of the meaning makers' past experience, current responses, and select personality characteristics. This "lived reality" also consists of the meaning makers' awareness, understanding, interpretation, emphasis or attitude, and emotional state toward the context at hand. In order to better understand the "indivisible unity of personal characteristics and situational characteristics" present in this complex process, let's consider the similarities and differences in meaning making that capture Toño and Beto's lived experiences during a visit to the Science Park in the ethnographic accounts below (Vygotsky, 1994, p. 342).

A Day of Discovery at the Science Park

The sun peeked between wisps of clouds in an opaque, pearl sky. Although the pastel yellow ball began its ascent a few hours earlier, the dry morning heat already created mirages above the pavement. The sounds of the city seemed distant and muted. Gradually, singing tires, squeaking crane cables, and the rustle and rumble of steel trucks hurtling across concrete overpasses shook families and businesses from their summer slumber. A solitary bird chirped from a willow tree as the small group assembled, meeting at the entrance of the Science Park. Juana, Miranda, and I waited patiently for the gates to open for Beto and Toño to experience a day of exploration and discovery with Teresa and Marisol.

Beto's Adventure at the Science Park

Beto tugged down on his big blue baseball cap as he sat quietly beside his mother. There was not enough room for everyone on the bench, so the child squeezed halfway onto her lap to make room for Miranda and Tere. Quietly and contentedly, Beto carefully removed a set of mirrored sunglasses from his pocket. He gently faced the eyewear toward him, tenderly inspecting the gift. His oldest brother had purchased the delicate glasses for today's outing. Beto tilted the lenses forward until he could see Tere in their reflection. Reading his finely tuned actions, the middle-schooler momentarily stopped licking her lollipop to briefly stick out her tongue at her little brother. The two quietly giggled, sharing a private laugh as the youngest members of their family. Beto gingerly returned the glasses to his pocket, smiled, and whispered to his mother. The two smiled at each other. Beto commenced sitting silently with one hand in his pocket. The family waited in a comfortable silence while park personnel unchained the jingling gates to the admission counter.

Today was a special day for Beto because his *Maestra* was taking his family to the Science Park. His mother told him he had visited a zoo once in Mexico City when Beto was three, but he could not remember being there. Tere explained the Science Park was better because there were also machines, play equipment, science materials, and computer games to explore. After visiting the Science Park with her fourth grade class, his older sister related she had seen turtles bigger than the family's kitchen table. When he laughed at Tere's assertion, his father corrected Beto stating that, in various parts of the world, turtles grew so large that they would not fit inside the boy's plastic pool on the driveway.

Since that day, Beto was desperate to see the giant turtles at the Science Park. When I first told Beto we would visit the site, the generous son was so excited, he asked if his whole family could join us. Despite the 100-degree temperature and Miranda's size in her third trimester of pregnancy, both women joined Beto and Tere as a demonstration of support for the youngest Chavez member. Suddenly, a voice announced in English and Spanish that the park was open for visitors. At long last, Beto eagerly stood up from the bench. His mother stood behind him in line, gently touching his shoulder when it was his turn to proffer the ticket admitting the shy little boy to the park.

Just inside the entrance, coral flamingos stood guard in a pool, resting on delicate stilt legs. Their necks and hooked black beaks drooped downwards in a tangled assortment of pink curves. A pair of cheerful brown ducks emerged from a clump of rushes with a trail of babies in their wake. As Beto walked along the water's edge, he pointed to the rapid paddle of their orange, webbed feet, betraying their seamless movement. Tere suggested we visit the indoor exhibits before the thick crowds arrived, so our group rushed toward a large wooden building with colorful banners of animals posted on the outside. Beto laughed at the funny peacocks on the path. The birds' head feathers bobbed furiously as the awkward, funky creatures sought refuge in the woodchips along the path as our party advanced upon them.

Tere ran up a long, brown plank to a huge, wooden door. *La Maestra* heaved open the tall barricade and ushered everyone inside. Beto found himself within a large room filled with giant skeletons. The walls were painted to look like brown caves and rocks. Beto followed his mother closely as the party made its way past glass cases with long, pointed teeth, purple rocks, and white cards with letters on them. His teacher pointed out the skeleton on the other side of the room once belonged to a Tyrannosaurus Rex like the plastic dinosaur toy he played with at school. The little boy gulped and squeezed his eyes shut. At Tere's urging, Beto looked up to observe the wingspan of an enormous bat-like skeleton hanging from the ceiling. Frowning, he reached for Miranda's hand and kept his eyes firmly fixed to the floor. Beto was afraid if he looked too long, the pterodactyl bones would return to him on *el día de los muertos*.

The little boy was greatly relieved when Tere guided the assembly to another room with life-sized photos of animals and stuffed bears, beavers, zebras, and mountain lions with real fur. Juana helped her son measure his height against a poster of a leg of an African elephant. Beto chatted with Miranda as he touched the textures and designs of animal furs next to life-sized photographs of their owners. He wandered wide-eyed among the stuffed beasts. In the center of the room, the reserved child stopped and watched a little girl create impressions of a deer running with rubber animal tracks inside a large, open sand tray. Beto had just selected a turtle stamp of his own when Miranda called him over to a three-foot, black stand in the corner of the room.

As Beto approached the case, a look of wonder crossed his face. Resting his hands gently on the top of the glass, the little boy peered down at a blue turtle carved from lapis stone about the size of a large dinner plate. The sculpture was inlaid with precious green, purple, and coral stones. Beto's mouth opened slightly as his eye traced the lines of gold that contoured the artist's handiwork. Both Tere and Toño shouted to him from a door on the other side of the room. Ignoring their pleas, the child calmly requested, "Mamá, saca un foto." His mother obliged, snapping a picture of Beto in front of the case. With a skip, Beto turned and walked through the doorway where his sister and classmate had disappeared.

Inside, the child was visually bombarded by multiple exhibits. Checking to see if Miranda and Juana were following closely, the little boy wandered among displays of spinning planets, swinging pendulums, and multicolored, electronic boards showing the oxygenation of blood in the circulatory system. Amidst over thirty displays, Beto spotted a giant light board with a circular grid over its surface. Pulling up a stool, the boy poked yellow, red, blue, and green pegs into the framework, smiling as each color illuminated their respective slots. Beto had created a geometric pattern from different colored lines when Tere reappeared to accompany him to the bubble chamber.

Brother and sister waited patiently for five minutes or more while another family played with the bubble maker. When it was their turn, the two children stepped into an enormous truck tire that had been split in half. A giant hula-hoop ring floated within a sea of sudsy, bubble fluid inside the tire. Tere pulled down on an overhead rope attached to a system of pulleys that served as a lever for the ring. Slowly, the hoop rose out of the tire enveloping the children inside a spectacular bubble. Suddenly, in an instant, the iridescent dome popped, releasing tiny twinges of liquid where the bubble vanished before the child's eyes. Beto shrieked with delight.

Tere lowered the ring into the tire a second time, challenging Beto to shut his eyes and keep his arms tucked tightly at his sides. Tere slowly pulled the cord as the children eagerly anticipated the moment the rope would advance no further. When the pulley jammed, the brother and sister opened their eyes. A seven-foot, opalescent tower surrounded them, refracting the colors of the room. Beto and Tere took turns maneuvering the cords and levers for approximately fifteen minutes. The two children experimented with the speed at which they pulled the cord, the resulting height of the bubble, and the length of time the delicate prism lasted before exploding into air with their laughter. When a small line began to form in front of the exhibit, the thoughtful siblings agreed to move on to the next building.

Outside, the brilliant sun reached its zenith and danced in aquamarine ripples of the polar bear exhibit. Beto carefully retrieved the gift from his pocket, placing the mirrored sunglasses on his nose. Hanging both arms over a chain-link fence, the little boy gazed down at the wet, white and grey bears frolicking over an ice block in the deep blue water. Beto was watching the show through his shades when Toño scooted over to him. The two bears played with the large, white square. When the smaller of the two animals successfully wrapped its arm over the top of the bobbing ice, his larger companion splashed its two giant paws, sending the desired object to the other side of the pool.

"Un oso," remarked Beto. "Mira ese grandote."

"Dah!" Toño exclaimed as the smaller animal swam across the pool, chasing the floating block.

Beto laughed and pointed, "Mira, mira el chiquito. Es chiquito."

Toño chuckled and replied, "Baby bear." Beto nodded in agreement as a third polar bear scaled the top of the rock, peering down at the water.

"Look it," Beto noted in English. Toño replied to his friend, "Momma bear. Dat's funny!" Calling down to the furry white creatures wrestling over the giant ice cube, Toño cried, "Hello! You're a dad bear. You're a kid bear. Ha—see da bear down there?"

Beto tipped his chin toward the third bear crawling down to the pool. "Look at bear," he indicated. "Over there. Look at them."

Toño answered, "Yeah, that's a mom. No, wait—that's a kid. He's following his dad."

The two boys laughed. The furry creature jumped into the water, sending a huge splash over the other animals. "Look at that big one," Beto retorted. "*Hay era que...* look at dat."

Suddenly, Toño turned and walked away. Pulling the sunglasses down his nose, Beto distinguished between the difference in the bear's color with and without his lenses. He was grateful for the soothing impact the spectacles had against the intense glare of the sun.

Following a small path, the group walked down and around the side of a giant rock barricade to discover a second pool where brown, rubber-skinned seals sunbathed under a crashing fountain. Hot, tired, and hungry, Beto lagged behind until Tere located a rock enclosure leading to a view of the seals' underwater world. Resting his sweaty forehead against the cool window, the little boy wearily observed the sleek, smiling animals comically cruise by with belly and neck exposed, flapping their mighty wing-like flippers in a graceful prayer. Beto wished he could join the seals' silent, circular path in their serene, turquoise playground.

Beto was called out of his daydream by his classmate.

"C'mon!" Toño yelled. "We're going to the '*cu-a-ree-yo!*"

The polite and respectful boy was frustrated with Toño's behavior. Beto did not like the way Toño constantly yelled and rushed ahead of the group. The well-mannered child was confused and angered by his peer's interruptions and commands. Inside the aquarium, Beto distanced himself from Toño, eyeing the actions of his classmate with a resentful and judging eye. The dark, noisy building was freezing and smelled horrible. Beto could not hear anything except the grueling roar of echoing tank motors. Spooky eels and mean-eyed fish shot out from behind rocks, frightening the little boy. Beto understood the trapped creatures could not attack him, but he slipped his hand inside his mother's palm for safe measure.

Beto's stomach hurt. His ears rang and he felt irritated, insecure, and cold. He tried to talk to Toño, but the boy spoke too fast. A shark longer than his brother was tall loomed ghostlike above Beto in the big tank. The child shuddered, removed his sunglasses from his pocket, and handed them to his mother. Pulling off his baseball hat, Beto punched his fist repeatedly into its center. His teacher, sisters, and mother tried to switch his attention to a mammoth sea turtle, but Beto would not be diverted. He paced in front of the large shark tank until it was time for lunch.

The remainder of the Science Park was divided into a small zoo with African and North American exhibits. In keeping with the local geography, monumental sandstone barricades separated the animals and people who came to view them. Once outside, Beto returned to his usual, cheerful self. Shady, twisted cottonwood trees dotted open paths leading to small buildings with indoor/outdoor cages. Navajo willows graced the many flower displays fed by a tiny stream, meandering around the park. Patches of bleached wood, yucca, thistles, and cacti were arranged to remind the public to remain on the paved or woodchip paths.

Revived from lunch, Beto pointed out two dusty elephants showering themselves in a dark green pool behind a pine grove. Sporting his glasses, he paused in front of a jaguar's cage, mesmerized by the cat's incessant snarling and pacing. The little boy witnessed the screeching of marmosets and other monkeys swinging from dead trees protected by nets. He and Toño shared a hearty laugh when a bulky, horned rhinoceros urinated strongly for several minutes. Beto identified colorful toucans with the birds from his favorite cereal box. He snapped several pictures of a black, furry mother gorilla cradling her newborn, alone in the tall grass. Beto could not see the baby, but the park ranger told the group it was there.

As the descending sun took on a slightly golden light, Beto asked his mother to guard his sunglasses in her purse. The tired party entered the last exhibit area to be rudely shocked by the terrifying screech of a bald eagle from the top of a dead tree. The noble bird's neck was crooked, much like the icon on the Mexican flag. Its piercing eyes and golden beak turned side to side, scrutinizing Beto and the others. The boy took a step backwards to look at a visual display about the bird. Seeing a drawing of an eagle's talon, Beto shaped his hand in a claw-like position. His thoughts were interrupted by Tere's shouts, "*¡Beto, Beto! ¡Ven acá! ¡Ven acá!*" The little boy placed his hand on top of his cap and walked hurriedly towards his sister. "*¡Las tortugas!*" yelled his sister as she disappeared around the corner to a path below.

The polite boy had waited all day for this moment. Beto turned and glanced at his mother for permission. Juana nodded once, setting her tender-hearted son free. For the first time all day, the little boy ran at full speed away from the group, down a hillside to the sturdy, thatched pavilion where Tere stood waiting. Beto stopped and jumped straight up in the air twice, attempting to glimpse over the fenced barricade. Placing his hands on the bars, he frantically bobbed his head, searching grassy patches between the small palm trees and giant boulders of the exhibit. "*Umberto!*" his mother shouted. For a moment, it appeared Beto was going to cry. The urgency in her tone led the little boy immediately back up the path. Juana met her son halfway down the hill. Without a word, she turned his back so he faced out over an opening in the rocks and, leaning over, placed her chin on his shoulder. Taking his right hand in hers, Juana pointed both of their index fingers toward a greenish boulder cast in partial shade. A hot breeze blew gently. Mother and son stood very still.

Then suddenly, the rock moved. A greenish-brown land tortoise lumbered into the sunlight on log-like legs. Its dusty shell was the size of a small table top. Beto perched on top of the sandstone barricade just above his beloved friend. The creature's muscular neck extended slowly to root about the grass. As Beto sat down on top of his boulder, the turtle raised its ancient head. Silently, the little boy extended his right arm in back of him. His mother placed the sunglasses into Beto's open hand. The mother and child sat silently for an extended period of time. We left five minutes before the gift shop was to close and the shadows grew too long to see *la tortuga* at the end of the day.

Toño's Navigation of the Science Park

The sun peeked between wisps of clouds in an opaque, pearl sky. Although the pastel, yellow ball began its ascent a few hours earlier, the dry morning heat already created mirages above the pavement. The sounds of the city seemed distant and muted. Gradually, singing tires, squeaking crane cables, and the rustle and rumble of steel trucks hurtling across concrete overpasses shook families and businesses from their summer slumber. A solitary bird chirped from a willow tree as our small group assembled, meeting at the entrance of the Science Park .

Toño played with the sticky Velcro strip on his brown sandals as he sat beside his older sister. He repeatedly opened and closed the adhering strap over and over again until Marisol shooed him off the edge of the bench for soiling the knees of her clean, white jeans. As Toño waited impatiently for the admissions counter to open, the little boy traced his index finger along the outer edges of the tall, metal barricade. "Teacher, teacher," he complained to me. "When's it gonna open?"

Spotting a wooden rack filled with colorful papers and brochures, Toño ran over and removed a document from all twenty pockets. When his arms were full, Sol informed Toño in an irritated voice she had no intentions of carrying all his papers for the remainder of the day. Raising his eyebrows, Toño shoved all but one of the flyers back into a single slot. The little brother then walked back to the bench to deliberately step on Sol's pastel pink tennis shoes.

Toño had looked forward to returning to the Science Park. The child had traveled its tree-lined paths the summer before with his Tía Fabiola and Marisol. The active, inquisitive boy was happy to escape his hot, tiny home. Toño's parents had not allowed him to play outside with his trucks and army men since the little girl down the street had been killed. He was tired of sitting on the itchy couch watching cartoons all day; Toño was eager to see the ferocious sharks in the big tank again.

At first, Toño was angry when his mother said Marisol would accompany him to make sure he behaved himself. After vehement refusals and tearful crying, his older sister calmed him by promising to buy Toño a gift at the little Park Store if he was good all day. In the early morning quiet, the little boy now strained his eyes past iron bars to a small building with public bathroom signs. Colorful stuffed animals smiled in its windows.

Toño skipped back and forth in front of the entrance as the park personnel unchained jingling gates to the admission counter. He suddenly remembered the brochure in his left hand and slowed down for a minute to examine it. The slick, beige advertisement had a tiger, parrot, garden, and lots of letters on it. Toño roughly unfolded the top and bottom flaps, and opened the colorful document like a mariachi's accordion. Shifting his weight, Toño waved and shuffled the document to obtain a proper hold. The creased paper expanded to the size of a poster wider than the little boy's arms could stretch. "Hey!" Toño exclaimed to no one in particular. He surveyed a large picture with flat, one-dimensional roads, trees, and a little stream. The artist had placed colored animal heads next to little houses on the roads.

Suddenly, a voice announced in English and Spanish that the park was open for visitors. "I first! I first!" the little boy cried. Toño rushed to the turnstile to the front of the line. I switched places with him to purchase the park tickets, a woman in the booth above him leaned over and said in a friendly tone, "*Veo que tienes tu mapa, mijo.*"

Toño did not completely understand what the ticket attendant said, but his ears perked up at the word "mapa." He smiled back, presented the ticket I had handed him, and rushed into the park.

Just inside the entrance, coral flamingos stood guard in a pool resting on delicate, stilt legs. Their necks and hooked black beaks drooped downwards in a tangled assortment of pink curves. Toño sat down by the side of the pool, critically examining the map in his hands while the rest of our group entered the park one at a time. This map was different than the ones he drew of buried treasure in his front yard. The little boy identified the roads as sidewalks and the tiny heads of giraffes, polar bears, and birds. As he searched for a shark, Beto's sister suggested the group visit the indoor exhibits before the thick crowds arrived. "C'mon," he urged. "Let's go!"

Toño folded his map in half and the group rushed toward a wooden building with colorful banners of animals swaying in the light breeze. He giggled as Beto laughed at the funny peacocks on the path ahead of them. As the party gained ground, the birds' head feathers bobbed furiously as the awkward, funky creatures sought refuge in the woodchips along the path.

Tere led us up a long, brown plank to a huge wooden door. I heaved open the tall barricade and ushered Toño inside. There was a large room filled with giant skeletons.The walls were painted to look like brown caves and rocks. Toño handed Sol his map and placed both hands on a cool, plaster column that connected the floor and ceiling. He recognized the strangely formed stalagmites and stalactites as cave furniture from his favorite cartoon. The sound of dripping water echoed from dusky corners. Sol admonished Toño to keep his hands to himself and attempted to return the map, but her little brother walked quickly into the center of the room. Sizing up the tremendous dinosaur spines surrounding him, Toño issued a hearty approval. "Look!" he cried to himself, "Look!" Charging toward a full mammoth skeleton with piercing tusks, the little boy shouted, "A bony elephant! A bony elephant!"

Toño stood directly underneath the display, rocking from side to side on each sandal. He talked to the skeleton, while laughing and waving his arms in the air. When Sol walked up behind him, the little boy took off running to a square, glass case a few feet away. Inside, Toño discovered long, pointed teeth, purple rocks, and white cards with writing on them. An array of geodes glistened under a bright spotlight like mummy treasure. Nearby, I pointed out that the skeleton on the other side of the room once belonged to a Tyrannosaurus Rex like the dinosaur toy he played with at school.

Sizing up the gigantic skull and jaw, Toño announced, "This is the big head dinosaur!" The child stood sideways next to the display to align his profile with the fated animal. Toño opened his left eye and jaw as wide as he was able and bared his sharp, white teeth like the skeleton. When Beto's mother giggled at Toño's private imitation of the skull, he laughed at himself and skipped ahead of Sol as the group moved toward the door of an adjoining room.

Inside, the inquisitive boy viewed life-sized photos of animals and stuffed bears, beavers, zebras, and mountain lions with real fur. Toño patted a gazelle on its smooth neck and moved into the middle of the room. There a little girl created impressions of a deer running with rubber animal track stamps inside a large, open sand tray. Toño traced lines in the sand with his forefinger until he glanced up and witnessed Sol examining a starfish under a microscope. He ran over and begged to look inside the long ocular tube his older brother had told him about from school.

Sol showed Toño how to move the knobs to focus the lens. The curious child rapidly moved the eyepiece up and down until he became dizzy. Sol pushed Toño aside, slowly tightened the knob, and then warned her brother not to touch the equipment as he peered a second time into the scope. Toño imagined he was a pirate discovering treasure as he peered into the lens. A wave of excitement crossed his face as he identified lines of geometric houses on a hill as the tan bumps from the starfish's arms. Toño leaned in to marvel at the interesting designs created by the sea creature's pores and striations otherwise invisible to the naked eye.

Hearing an unfamiliar voice call his name, Toño looked up to see Beto's sister pointing to another doorway. The little boy ran over to Teresa and shouted at his classmate to hurry up. "Da's enough guys," the impish child yelled. "Let's go!"

Toño entered the new room and was visually bombarded by multiple exhibits. He shouted with glee as he dodged from station to station, manipulating everything in his path. Toño jumped inside the driver's seat of a child-sized car and imitated the sound of a running motor and screeching brakes, while he jammed its steering wheel from side to side. The boy raced to a stand with a dulcimer and plucked the instruments' silver, fairy strings. Toño plopped down onto a stool in front of a play restaurant and pretended to order a hamburger. The active child rushed to a cardboard display of a blue-uniformed mailman and a chef wearing a red apron. Sticking his face through holes in the board, he insisted Sol take pictures of him as a postal worker and a cook.

The brother and sister noticed the bubble station at the same time. Laughing loudly, the two played swords with giant bubble wands over an elevated baby pool as they waited for a turn in the bubble chamber. When the line grew too long and the child realized he would have to wait with everyone else to earn a spot, Toño turned his attention to building a house from a large assortment of white plastic pipes. Ignoring another child who attempted to converse with him, Toño independently connected pipe after pipe for approximately fifteen minutes. When Beto and Tere finished at the bubble chamber, Toño and Sol met at the doors and agreed to move on to the next building.

Outside, the brilliant sun reached its zenith and danced in the aquamarine ripples of the polar bear exhibit. Hanging both arms over a chain-link fence, Toño gazed down at the wet, white and grey bears frolicking over an ice block in the deep blue water. Toño laughed as one of the polar bears floated on his back, while licking his right arm with a skinny, pink tongue. He scooted over to where Beto was watching the show through his sunglasses.

The two bears played with the large, white square of ice. When the smaller of the two animals successfully wrapped its arm over the top of the bobbing ice, his larger companion splashed its two giant paws sending the desired object to the other side of the pool.

"Un oso," remarked Beto. "Mira ese grandote."

"Dah!" Toño exclaimed as the smaller animal swam across the pool, chasing the floating block.

Beto laughed and pointed, "Mira, mira el chiquito. Es chiquito."

Toño chuckled and replied, "Baby bear."

Beto nodded in agreement as a third polar bear scaled the top of the rock, peering down at the water.

"Look it," Beto noted in English.

Toño replied to his friend, "Momma bear. Dat's funny!"

Calling down to the furry white creatures wrestling over the giant ice cube, Toño cried, "Hello! You're a dad bear. You're a kid bear. Ha—see da bear down there?"

Beto tipped his chin toward the third bear crawling down to the pool. "Look at bear," he indicated behind his glasses. "Over there. Look at them."

Toño answered, "Yeah, that's a mom. No, wait—that's a kid. He's following his dad."

The two boys laughed. The furry creature jumped into the water, sending a huge splash over the other animals.

"Look at that big one," Beto retorted. "*Hay era que*...look at dat."

Suddenly, Toño remembered his map. Whining loudly, Toño stamped his feet when Sol related she had asked me to carry the document in my bag.

Following a small path, our group walked down and around the side of a giant rock barricade to discover a second pool where brown, rubber-skinned seals sunbathed under a crashing fountain. Toño chased after me, tapping my purse as he repeatedly begged for his map. We sat down at a bench in front of a rock enclosure.

Opening the document, I traced the route our group had walked since arriving at the park. The intelligent little boy drew a connection between the bear and seal icons and the location of our bench on the park map. At that moment, Toño realized the animal heads identified which creatures lived in the various exhibits along the park paths. Pointing to the symbol of a seal on a rock, the child drew a line from the seal to a fish. The little boy instantly grew excited at his discovery. "The fish-house! The fish-house!" he cried.

Laughing, I replied, "Yes, that's the aquarium. Your grandma and grandpa call it *el acuario* in Spanish." Toño had searched the map looking for a shark instead of a fish icon.

The happy boy dashed over to Beto who was pressing his face against the cool glass, watching underwater seals at play. "C'mon!" he yelled. "We're going to the *cu-a-ree-yo!*"

Beto's mother turned and smiled at the excited little boy. Juana spoke directly to Toño in Spanish as she toussled his hair. Toño smiled back, and responded "Chic-em, gutierrez."

Juana and Marisol laughed kindly at his Spanish-sounding nonsense words. Toño momentarily placed his hand in Juana's palm as the mother and two classmates walked to the middle of the sidewalk. Pulling out his map, Toño identified the fish symbol on the document with the corresponding sign posted in front of the aquarium. Thrilled with his newfound competence, the little boy raced to open the doors for the party, urgently persuading the group to hurry into the dark, freezing building.

As his shouts echoed over the roar of tank motors, Toño pleaded, "Let's check sharks are doing. Let's check sharks are doing."

The boy proceeded up a ramp to a large, circular, standing pool with an open top. Miniature, bat-like rays leaped and dove across the surface of the water. "Da sharks flying!" shrieked the little boy.

"That's a stingray," I noted in English.

"Stingray. Whoaaaaa!" replied Toño. He turned to advise his older sister, "See that stingray. Hey—look at that stingray. Dat stingray. It sting fishes."

"Could it sting anything else?" I probed.

"Think only fishes," responded the little boy. Admiring the movement of the triangular-shaped animals, Toño added, "He some smart *pez.*" The curious child shifted his attention. "Hey! Let's go. Never mind the stingers."

Toño scurried ahead down a dark hallway illuminated by the torquoise-yellow glow of several small tanks embedded in the concrete walls. Purple, green, and brown plants waved in slow motion on tiny landscapes of brilliantly colored gravel. Toño ran down the corridor in a zig-zagged line from window to frame. "Look at this, teacher! Look!" he cried at each station.

"What kind of fish do you see?" I inquired. Toño peered at a school of tiny green minnows.

"I don't know," the child stated. "Bean-fish? Bean-fish are—um—small and big fish."

Racing to a tank of baby piranhas, Toño importantly announced, "These are chasing-fish!" The creative boy identified several other species using the descriptive names of bird-fish, smoke-fish, orange-fish, horse-fish, Conner-fish, flying-fish, and slow-fish. Toño delighted in watching a small lobster parade along a sandy floor like a tiny, battery-operated truck.

As Toño reached the end of the hallway, his eyes fell upon a great salt water tank with colorful creatures of all shapes, textures, and sizes. The inquisitive boy passed back and forth in front of the glass, searching the turquoise depths for a stealthy shadow.

"Deres da shark!" he yelled, spotting a pointed nose and fin. "Deres it! Deres da same shark. I wanna see him!" Toño started to advance toward an adjoining room.

"No, let's wait. Let's slow down a minute. What kind—what color fish do you see?" I asked.

Toño replied, "I see green fish."

"Green? And only green?" I encouraged. Toño was not so easily deterred. "Here," I said, pointing to a coral reef. "Here we've got our blue fish and we've got grey fish..."

"What about da shark?" Toño demanded. I ignored him and continued, "We've got pink fish and..."

"A zebra fish," Sol interjected. A tiny clown fish rushed out from behind a sea urchin.

"Look!" Toño shouted. "I like! Look! A orange fish!" But, the child pressed on. "Let's go to the shockers-senders," he urged. "Hey—we'll all go to the shockers-senders!"

Our group reluctantly succumbed to the wishes of the self-selected tour guide. Turning the corner, we walked into a short room with two enormous, obelisk-shaped tanks. Purple and white jelly-fish swam in circles like ghostly UFOs. An adjoining hallway led to a shark tank the size of a large room.

As Toño entered the ocean landscape, he let out a squeal of delight. He ran up to the invisible wall, placing his forehead against the glass with both arms balanced above him. Brown, sand-tiger, black tip, and nurse sharks emerged from bubbled shadows. Only a few feet separated the small boy from the creatures of the vast cold, blue waters. A lime-green sea turtle waved hello in slow motion as Toño laughed and waved back. Searching among the ancient grey predators, Toño chose the shark with the largest teeth and whispered hello. He continued a conversation with his ferocious friend until it was time for lunch.

According to Toño's map, the remainder of the Science Park was divided into a small zoo with African and North American exhibits. In keeping with the local geography, monumental sandstone structures separated the animals and people who came to view them. Toño directed his friends amidst the shady, twisted cottonwood trees dotting the open paths. Referring to his map, the child accurately announced what exhibits the group approached well within view of the buildings' indoor/outdoor cages.

When the bright child didn't know the name for an animal's icon on the document, Toño invented a verbal label based on the creature's physical or behavioral characteristics. Navajo willows graced the many flower displays fed by a tiny stream that meandered around the park. Patches of bleached wood, yucca, thistles, and cacti prevented Toño from forging novel venues between the routes on his chart and the paved or woodchip paths.

Fatigued from the sun and a full lunch, Toño wandered past two dusty elephants showering themselves in a dark green pool underneath a pine grove. The insistent child directed the group to a parrot cage where he snapped a photograph of two birds with lush green feathers accented with red and gold. Referring to his map, Toño urged the party past the odiferous wild cat and monkey cages to visit the rhinoceros exhibit. He and Beto shared a hearty laugh when the bulky, horned beast urinated strongly for the duration of several minutes. By the time the group approached the gorilla exhibit, Toño had fallen uncharacteristically quiet. He trudged along the park trail with his face hidden behind the oversized map. Absorbed by the features in the document, Toño spoke to himself while the rest of the group snapped pictures of a black, furry mother gorilla cradling her newborn alone in the tall grass.

As the descending sun took on a slightly golden light, Beto's oldest sister, Miranda, mentioned in Spanish she needed to visit the ladies' room. Toño's ears perked up. "*Baño*," he repeated, pointing to the map's blue restroom icons at the entrance to the park.

The young, pregnant woman smiled at him warmly. "I'll show her where it is," the little boy chirped importantly.

"Don't you want to see the rest of the animals?" I asked. "We only have half an hour left."

The tired little boy slowly shook his head. "Sol can go with us, too," he offered in an overly friendly manner.

I peered at the map and considered Toño's mischievous smile. The restrooms were located next to the icon denoting the Science Park store. Our group caught up with the trio outside the gift shop. They were happily catching drips from forbidden ice cream cones as the clank of chains across bars reminded us the park was closing. Toño stood up, tucking his map under one arm and his new stuffed jelly fish under the other, ready for the next adventure.

Capturing Meaning in Text

A ll peoples have developed symbolic systems to share emotion, generate and relate ideas, retell the past, and project the future. Cultural approaches to literacy have ranged widely across time, geography, and technologies: We have created diverse symbolic systems from a host of physical and psychological tools including Incan counting knots, Slavic birch marks, and the iPad to recount meanings of and from our life experiences.

Oral language originated from our collective need to work in groups as members of families, communities, and larger society. Reading and writing systems further afforded the opportunity to participate in relationships with others in their ability to relate the transparent and transitory nature of thought and speech. Written speech provided a bridge that transcends place and time to preserve and communicate our perezhivanie. Because our lived experience—lives, loves, traditions, values, customs, questions, strategies, problem solving, aspirations, and dreams—are captured in text, membership in many cultures is achieved by the acquisition of distinct linguistic or literate practices.

Emergent Biliteracy:
Learning to Coordinate Physical and Psychological Tools

A combination of physical (books, charts, pencils) and psychological tools (algorithms, languages, and writing systems) permit us to co-construct and mediate knowledge or understandings (Mahn, 1997). Because "knowledge is not internalized directly, but through the use of psychological tools," the task of childhood is to discover, acquire and re-create the tools of meaning-makers from the preceding generation (John-Steiner and Mahn, 1996, p. 193; Cole, 1996).

Children and other learners successively coordinate these physical and psychological tools with the help of more advanced peers and adults. Meaning making practices, including biliteracy, develop our minds and higher thought processes (Vygotsky, 1986). When emergent biliterates like Toño and Beto tap into their dual linguistic reservoirs, both their thoughts and indentities are shaped and transformed (Vygotsky, 1981). Let's take a look at how the children capture the significance of their perezhivaija or lived experiences at the Science Park with both physical and psychological tools in texts that are meaningful to them.

El Superhéroe Beto

A few days after our visit to the Science Park, in the craft room at the local public library, Beto lifted his tiny hands to his chin and casually propped his elbows against the large wooden table. Slowly turning his small head from left to right, the little boy quietly considered each of the individual photographs before him. Beto's brown eyes slowly danced over the huge array of colorful pictures. After three or four minutes of comfortable silence, the contented child's mouth broke into a toothless grin. Reaching across the table to select a snapshot, a look of delight spread across Beto's petite face like a private sunrise. Holding the print in front of me, the little boy announced, "*Esta.*"

"This one?" I repeated, matching his broad smile. Beto subtly nodded, passed me the photograph, and placed both hands over his mouth to contain a shy giggle.

I smiled myself, peering closely at the picture. Presented with the task of choosing one snapshot out of a collection of fifty to frame for his mother and father, Beto opted for a scene near and dear to his heart. The image captured a sea turtle the size of a salad plate, frozen in motion inside a sparkling tank. The dark, green creature was closely followed by two miniature babies, struggling to catch up with their mother. When I suggested Beto's parents might enjoy a print of him and his older sister, the loving son listened respectfully, smiled sweetly, then shook his head adamantly. After Beto placed the treasured photograph into the frame, he sat back in his chair, grinned at the gift, and nodded toward me gratefully.

I wondered what images the future herpetologist might include in the book we would create with pictures taken during our visit to the Science Park. Opening a large blue folder, I described to Beto how we'd use the heavy material to cover and bind a text of his own imagination. I explained the smart boy could pick any of the snapshots on the table to illustrate his story. I modeled how the child might select a print, glue it to the center of a page, and dictate words to me in the same manner we composed books during the school year. Finally, I showed Beto how he would tape the written dictation on the paper so I knew where to type his words when I assembled the final book on my computer at home. The little boy's eyes lit up when I suggested he give his published product as a second present to his family.

Placing the blue folder in front of the child, I asked Beto what photograph he wanted to paste on the front cover. The good natured boy stood up from his chair, gripped the table's edge with both hands, and leaned forward to view the display of pictures. Silently, Beto spied an image, smiled widely, and chose a picture of himself and Tere resting against a sandstone rock. Without speaking, the calm child softly laid the snapshot on top of the folder, turning to glance at me with an inquisitive look.

Touching the print with my right hand, I addressed the little boy. "What is the name of your book?" I prompted in Spanish. "¿El título?"

Beto hesitantly shrugged his small shoulders, pursed both lips tightly together, and spun his torso away from me to the right. Collapsing his hands in his lap, the little boy threw back his head, closed his eyes, and sat in a strained silence. After a few moments passed, Beto issued a barely audible, uncertain "Hmmm." He pretended to examine the tiles on the ceiling above him. I waited patiently for his words to come.

After a few more humming gestures, the child started to kick his chair. Beto turned his head toward me with his face parallel to the floor. I thought for a second the eager child was going to rest his head in my lap as I had seen Beto do with his mother. As I patted the back of his head, the little boy slowly sat up. "¿Los...?" the reluctant child initiated, then faltered.

"The...," I echoed. Pointing to his selected photograph I offered in Spanish, "The two children? The brother and sister?"

Beto sat up quickly in his seat and stated quickly, "Los dos primos!"

Nudging the picture a second time, I questioned the little boy in his first language. "Cousins? Are you and Tere cousins?"

Beto shook his head quizzically and observed me intently. I pointed to the snapshot a third time.

"What about a story called The Brother and Sister? Or, The Adventures of Beto and Tere?" I suggested.

Beto placed his right hand inside the left sleeve of his shirt. Smiling eagerly, the happy child nodded. Without talking, the little boy leaned close to me and softly chuckled. Wanting to hear Beto's own voice, I proposed another title. "Los Superhéroes Beto y Teri?"

The excited boy sat up in his seat. "Las Adventuras de Superhéroes Beto y Tere," he announced proudly.

Hiding his mouth briefly with his shirt sleeve, Beto stuck the fabric into his teeth. I began to articulate each word of his title out loud, deliberately matching the verbal and written sign on paper. "*Las ad-ven-tur-as...,*"I wrote. Pulling his shirt out of his mouth, Beto glanced up and nodded approvingly in silence.

"You tell me," I urged in Spanish. "*Las adventuras de...*"

The little boy slid backwards in his chair, sat up straight, and repeated in a formal tone, "*Las Adventuras de Superhéroes Beto y Tere.*"

As I finished encoding the remainder of the title in Spanish and English, Beto smiled emphatically.

"*¡Bueno!*" I validated in Beto's first language."Now we need to write the author's name like the other books we have written together. Who is this story written by?" I inquired.

Beto tucked his arms into his sides and looked away to the right side of the room. The little boy shut his eyes and mouth tightly, tipped his head backwards, and issued an extended, "Hmmmmm."

I silently crunched my toes and slowly counted to thirty in my head. At thirty-one, Beto opened his left eye and positioned his right index finger vertically across his lips. The humming sound resumed. At forty, Beto turned his torso and looked up expectantly at my face.

"Who is the author of your book, *mijo?*" I asked in Spanish. "Who is writing *The Adventures of the Superheroes Beto and Tere?*" The little boy leaned three inches forward to gaze at me intently.

I softly touched his left shoulder, whispering, "*Tú.*"

Beto searched my eyes and restated hopefully, "*Tú.*"

Gently tickling his stomach, I advised in Spanish,"You! You are writing the story! So, you are the author! I'm just helping you today."

In a flourish, I dramatically pointed to the title and read, "*The Adventures of the Superheroes Beto and Tere!*" Grabbing my pen and paper, I spoke and wrote in an exaggerated fashion, "*Por Umberto Chavez!*" Beto laughed out loud. After Beto taped his title and name to the folder, we reread the cover of his book together.

Next, I placed a sheet of paper in front of the little boy. I asked Beto in Spanish which photograph he wanted to glue down for the first page of his story. The eager child stretched across the pile of pictures to secure a print. "*Esa,*" he stated, positioning a snapshot of himself posed in front of a black stand with a glass case.

"Okay," I validated in his first language. "And what would you like to write about the print?"

Beto quietly leaned back in his chair, examining the photograph underneath the table. He suddenly smiled to himself, then tucked his lips inside his mouth. The mindful child slowly rocked his shoulders back and forth as he bobbed his head up and down. After an extended period of silence, the uncertain child turned his back to me.

"*Pues, a ver,*" I offered.

Beto leaned back in his chair and paused for a minute, uttering another, "Hmmm." Eventually, he made a circle with his torso and turned to present the picture to me. We gazed down at the handsome child standing by the encased turtle carving.

"What are you doing in the snapshot?" I prompted in Spanish.

Beto responded, "En frente de la tortuga azul."

"What kind of turtle is it?" I probed.

"*De joya,*" replied Beto.

"Maybe we can write, 'This is...,'" I started to suggest in the child's first language.

"*La tortuga de joya!*" Beto strongly concluded.

Praising the little boy, I repeated, "This is the jeweled turtle" in Spanish and English while copying his dictation onto a strip of paper. Beto painstakingly glued the selected print onto the page. After taping the sentence strip below the photograph, we read his dictation together in both languages. The happy child grinned as he inserted the first page within the blue folder.

"What about the second page?" I inquired in Spanish, arranging a blank paper before the little boy.

Beto rested both arms on top of the page. Closing his eyes and mouth, the quiet child turned his head to the left and inhaled deeply. Several moments passed without conversation before Beto shot an inquiring look at me.

"Las fotos, mijo. ¿Cual quieres usar?" I cued the little boy.

Beto stood up, wiped his nose on his sleeve, and placed the inside of his right hand over his chin. Chewing on his thumb, the child produced a soft "Hmmm" while he thoroughly scanned the pictures from side to side.

Instantly, Beto's face lit up. Leaning across the table, he selected a snapshot and placed it in the center of the page. "*¿Esta?*" the little boy questioned.

Beto had selected a print of himself inside the bubble chamber at the Science Park. In the photograph, a giant iridescent column surrounded the laughing child as he pulled on a rope.

"Great!" I reassured him in Spanish. "And what is happening in the picture?"

The little boy responded, "*Estoy adentro un globo.*"

All of a sudden, Beto began to slide off his chair. The athletic child stopped himself from falling directly onto the floor by bracing both hands against the table. For a moment, Beto and I exchanged a look of horror. Reading the comical expression on each other's faces, we simultaneously started to laugh.

Giggling, the little boy then dictated, "*Estoy adentro un globo.*"

"Did you want me to write that for you?" I asked the merry child. Beto nodded appreciatively and rocked his shoulders up and down in his chair. The little boy continued to chuckle as he glued the snapshot onto the page.

"*Es-toy a-den-tro...,*" I emphasized each syllable while I recorded the child's dictation.

"*De...,*" supplied Beto as he worked alongside me.

"*De...un glo-bo,*" I repeated, finishing the sentence.

After we read the Spanish dictation together, I asked my young friend if he wanted to translate the sentence into English. Beto nodded eagerly and smiled.

"I am inside...," I began while I scripted the words.

"A bubble," the little boy finished in English.

"You got it!" I exclaimed, and the child smiled proudly.

After Beto secured his dictation to the sheet, we reread the cover and the first two pages together. This time, when I positioned a third paper in front of the child, the little boy stood up and surveyed the prints without any prompting.

"Hmmm...," he mused in a contemplative tone. This verbal gesture sounded differently than his previous utterances. Beto had straightened his posture and appeared to execute his movements with more confidence. After a few minutes of quiet deliberation, the wise child pushed aside a photograph to discover a hidden picture of himself sitting on top of a large, sandstone rock. "*Hay!*" he pronounced immediately.

A joyful laugh filled the room. Beto closely examined the snapshot of himself scrambling to obtain a better view of the turtle exhibit. "*Esta,*" he stated definitively, waving the print in the air.

The pleased child bobbed his head up and down while he glued the photograph onto the center of his third page. Beto lifted his feet in an unconscious march as we reread the text in its entirety.

"What do you want to write for your third page?" I inquired in Spanish.

A mischievous grin crept over the edge of the little boy's mouth. Placing his hand over his lips, Beto attempted to restrain a giggle. A chuckle escaped from inside the child's palm. We glanced at each other and laughed at the same time.

Still giggling, Beto eyed his third page and placed his hands together in front of his mouth. The little boy's fingertips briefly touched his lips as he struggled to swallow his merriment. For a moment, Beto assumed a serious expression, intoning, "*Voy a saltar por las tortugas.*" His statement was followed by a peal of laughter as the silly child reveled in his own joke.

Playing along with his game in Spanish, I held up the page, begging the child in the photograph, "No! No! Beto, don't go with the turtles! Please don't leave me here alone!" The little boy doubled over with laughter in his chair.

With his dictation recorded in both languages, Beto's eyes twinkled as he searched the array of pictures for his fourth page. He cupped his mouth with both hands to prevent random giggles from emanating between his fingers. Several minutes passed. The smart child returned to the section of the table where he first identified the previous snapshot.

Beto's silent laughter erupted when he located a second print of himself perched above the turtle exhibit. With eyes sparkling, the excited child displayed the photograph an inch from my face jubilantly announcing, "*¡Apena a saltar por la tortuga!*"

"Dying to jump in with the turtle," I teased in his first language. "Dying to go?! Don't do it, Beto! Please, please! Don't leave me!" I implored the picture in jest.

The little boy placed an arm over his chair to steady himself from laughing so hard. We giggled together as Beto glued the snapshot down and I translated his dictation into English.

Teasing the little boy in Spanish, I commented "I think you are in love with turtles!"

Beto nodded vigorously. "*Loco por tortugas!*" he added with a playful chortle.

"Pues, Senor Tortuga," I jested. "*¿Te gustan los gusanos?*"

The little boy searched my face wondering why I would ask him if he liked worms.

"Well, turtles eat worms," I explained in his first language. "I think you should eat a worm sandwich for lunch!"

Beto leaned back against his chair, gathering his knees to his chest. The playful child buried his face in his knees as his shoulders convulsed with spasms of hilarity.

We continued to joyfully construct Beto's book. In between pasting, dictating, translating, writing, and rereading, we joked with each other. In an hour's time, Beto's text included an additional photo of the little boy and his sister sitting near the seals. Three subsequent pages presented a rhino, seal, and shark accompanied by the repetitive phrase, "Yo veo un_____ ." or "I see a _____." The child's love for electronic games was reflected in two individual pages where he described his actions at the light board and a computer using "I" statements. Like a beach ball submersed underwater, our laughter resurfaced when the little boy characterized two photographs of himself and Tere inside the bubble chamber as worms and mice.

Sensing the child's waning attention, I decided to draw our session to a close. "OK, *Señor Superhéroe Tortuga*," I jovially conceded in Spanish. "One more page and we'll be finished."

Beto's chair made a scraping sound as the little boy stood up and folded his arms across his tiny chest. He straightened his posture and issued a very exaggerated, "Hmmm..." The little boy dramatically lifted his right index finger across his mouth. Attempting to conceal a smile, Beto turned his face sharply to the right away from me. His shoulders shook silently. The playful child marched heavily around the opposite side of the table, struggling to avoid eye contact.

Beto quickly snatched a photograph and held it to his stomach to hide it from view. Smothering a giggle with one hand, the little boy held his breath and fought to retain his composure as he slid back to his seat. In an explosion of laughter, the hysterical child displayed a third photo of himself scaling the rock above the turtle exhibit. When he could hold back no longer, Beto shrieked, "*¡Me voy a saltar por las tortugas y dormirme!*"

"What?" I earnestly inquired, pen in hand. I could not decipher the child's breathless outburst. After his belly laugh subsided, the little boy removed his hand from his stomach and turned to me with shining eyes. "*Maestra*," he dictated in English. "I am going to jump in with the turtles and go to sleep!"

Toño's Fish Tale

Toño taped a final button to the milk carton submarine he had been making. He carefully eyed his work, examining the creation from side to side. Marisol looked up from her own painting to complement her brother's efforts. Kneeling on his seat, the little boy turned to me and held out the delicate sculpture. "Done," he announced in a definitive tone.

I smiled to myself as I gingerly retrieved yet another project from Toño's impatient fingers. It was the third time I had heard the same phrase in little over an hour. Gently setting the fragile craft on the drying table, I recalled the little boy's excitement during our adventure at the Science Park two days ago. This afternoon on our way to the library, Toño had spoken animatedly about the creatures in the park's mini-aquarium.

Provided with a table of colorful supplies, unlimited assistance, and a wide choice of projects, Toño's artwork reflected the same intense interest of life underwater. The creative child had already drawn a scuba diver swimming in a shark tank and constructed a moray eel from multicolored sequins and tape. Glancing at the wobbly submersible, I noticed Toño included a tiny self-portrait in one of the ship's glue-smeared windows. Now as the little boy reached for a large piece of sky-blue cardboard, I wondered what the future oceanographer would construct next.

Toño surveyed the long craft table cluttered with books and art supplies. Markers, construction paper, glue, magazines, pipe cleaners, tissue, yarn, pom-poms, hangers, fish line, and all sorts of found objects invited his selection. Shuffling through a collection of colored papers, the little boy discovered a package of origami rice papers. He unwrapped the plastic and leafed through an assortment of squares representing all the colors of the rainbow. Placing green and orange papers to the right side of the table, Toño picked up a dark blue sheet with his right hand. After locating the scissors with his left hand, the intent child cut out the shape of a fish by sight.

The wrinkled figure sported a choppy silhouette with a round head and arrow tail. Spreading a dollop of paste in the center of the cardboard, Toño pressed his cutout into the milky liquid with two fingers from both hands. As he inspected its position on the page, the little boy announced in English, "This is a seaweed fish. One that hides."

Toño picked up a lime-green square and began cutting a second fish. As his tiny hands negotiated the utensil, the little boy elaborated, "He got sister."

"A sister?" I questioned, echoing Toño's statement.

Sticking his tongue against the inside of his right cheek to concentrate, the little boy continued to explain. "And some brothers."

Hoping the topic would develop into a story, I asked, "Does this seaweed fish play games with his brothers and sister?"

"No," Toño replied, considering the size of the page. "He won't have enough."

After gluing down the second fish in focused silence, Toño patted the new addition to the cardboard tank. Reversing hands and scissors, the child struggled to cut out an orange fish with his right hand.

"So," I said casually. "Do you want to write something about the seaweed fish?"

"Green," stated the little boy.

I extended my arm across the table and placed a plastic marker in front of my small friend. The busy child continued to cut as he shook his head. "Hey—I'm a call it Green," he explained. "The little sticker." Pointing to a page of file labels, Toño indicated he wanted me to write the name of the color on one of the white strips. "Green," he repeated. "Green is a lit-tle name," Toño stated as a matter of factly as he christened the fish.

I posed my pen above the solitary label. "Remember in school how we stretched out words like rubber bands? Grrr-eee-nnn. Gr—een." I pretended to pull an invisible rubber band in between my fingers as I enunciated the sounds of the word. "Grrr-een," I repeated. "Do you hear any letters that you know?"

Toño nodded and drew the letter G in the air. "Good! Any others? GR-een," I articulated.

" R!" shouted the little boy.

"Yes," I validated. "Green starts with a G and an R." I recorded the first two letters on the white sticker."Now listen again," I urged Toño. Sweeping my pen across the two written signs on the sticker, I pointed at the empty space to the right of the letter R. "Gr-EEE-NNN," I emphasized. "Gr-EEE-NNN."

"E and N—like my name," replied the smart boy.

"Yes," I praised him. "The 'E' said its name, didn't it? There are two E's in Green," I mentioned encoding the letters on the label. As I scripted the letter N, I confirmed, "You're right. The N is in your name, too."

I handed the completed sticker to Toño. The bright boy put down his scissors and placed the title underneath the green fish with both hands. "It's a baby one," he stated admiringly.

As Toño resumed cutting the orange fish with his left hand, I asked if he wanted to include a label with Green's name in Spanish. "Think so," quipped the child. "What is it?"

"Verde," I replied. "Verde is his Spanish name. It is spelled with a V but it sounds like a B."

Toño gestured to a second label and instructed me to cut it in half. As I divided the sticker, I slowly articulated the syllables and sounds in the word. Toño put down his scissors and reached for the glue. "Ber-de," he muttered to himself.

Using a process similar to the creation of the first label, I urged the creative child to help me sound and write verde as I recorded the written signs. Toño's final dictation included the Spanish letter-signs BRD with an English A substituting for the final Spanish *E*. The little boy placed the label above his green fish on the cardboard.

As Toño secured the title, he inquired, "What is orange-fish, teacher?"

"*Un pez anaranjado*," I answered, laughing at the look of surprise that registered on his face hearing the multisyllabic length of the word.

The selective child browsed through the remaining origami sheets. Copper, silver, and gold squares shimmered at the back of the stack. Marisol leaned forward and commented, "How pretty."

Fingering a gold foil square between his right thumb and forefinger, Toño exclaimed, "I wanna make a golden. I'm a call him Lucky." The little boy proceeded to cut a large, backwards S in the center of the shiny paper. A seahorse slowly emerged under the child's scissors.

"Did you want me to write anything for you, Toño?" I queried.

"Goldie's a tiny name," the child suggested.

"Goldie—that's a great idea!" I replied.

"Goldie," Sol echoed. "The lucky fish. No—the lucky seahorse." Toño's sister giggled as she corrected herself. "He's the luckiest seahorse in the ocean!"

"De toda la mar," I agreed.

Toño glued his sparkling seahorse to the left of the small school of fish. He stood up at the table and selected a green marker. The young artist quickly sketched long blades of wavy seaweed on either side of the creatures. Toño rapidly drew a floor of gravel using a variety of colors. Capping the markers, the little boy reached for the page of white labels and knelt on top of the seat on his chair.

As he opened a thin black marker, Toño noted the size of the stickers. "It's a small name like this small one," the child cheerfully observed. I assured him the seahorse's name would fit on the label. Toño looked up at me and asked, "How's start the /l/?"

The little boy was requesting help in remembering how to form the letter L. Pulling my chair closer, I leaned forward so Toño could observe the way I pronounced the creature's name. "/G/–/g/– Goldie," I articulated, emphasizing the initial consonant. "/G/– can you hear the letter G?" I probed.

"Yeah," Toño retorted. "I know that G." The little boy affirmed how to construct the written sign. Toño slowly inscribed a capital G on the small label with his left hand. The child then paused and looked at me for the next cue.

"G–O-ldie. G–O-ldie," I pronounced, accenting the long /o/ sound. "What letter name do you hear?"

Toño quickly wrote the sign for a capital O next to the G on the label. "The end of my name," he murmured under his breath.

"Yes! TO-ñO. GO. Gol-die," I rhymed. Recalling his sentence strings from the child's newspapers and advertisements from the previous spring, I secretly crossed my fingers, wondering if the little boy was ready to transition into writing full words other than his name. "Go-L-die," I persisted stressing the third sign in the seahorse's name. "What comes next?"

Toño propped his elbow on the table and placed his cheek against the heel of his hand. The creative child frowned. I sang our chant for the letter L from the school year, outlining the capital letter in the air. The instant I began to form the sign in space, the little boy jumped out of his seat and stood up to write the letter. Toño glanced up from his writing. "Did it!" he smiled.

"Hey! Good job!" I cheered. "You have the first half of Gol-die. Now listen to the second part. Gol-DIE," I continued emphasizing the second syllable. As we restated the name, Toño and I gestured together as though we were stretching an unseen bungee cord. "What letter sounds do you hear in the second half of the word?" I inquired.

Bending his chin to the table, Toño turned his head sideways and stuck his tongue into his right cheek. The child's marker squeaked against the white label. The little boy concentrated intently as he inscribed the letters for a capital D and E. Sol and I clapped supportively. "Okay," I urged. "Read it to me."

Toño pointed to each sign as he matched the meaning, signs, and sounds in his fish's name. "G-O-L-D-E," he pronounced. This was the first time the little boy had composed and read the internal, grapho-linguistic structures in a single word of his own spelling. Toño placed the sticker on top of the seaweed above his seahorse.

"Okay," I pressed on. "Do you want to write Goldie's name in Spanish?" When the little boy nodded, I asked if he knew how to say the word in Spanish.

"Gol-da. Gol-da," the intelligent child pronounced with a strong New Mexican accent.

"Close!" I congratulated. "It's *Dorado. Dor-a–do.*"

"*Dor*," Toño enunciated as he scripted the capital letters D and R.

"*Dor– a–do*," I repeated, emphasizing the syllables in the name. Cuing the child, I suggested, "Remember your magic rubber band."

The little boy set down his marker and articulated the second and third syllables as he pretended to pull an invisible, elastic cord. A look of excitement passed quickly over his face. Leaning forward, Toño painstakingly recorded the D and O signs to complete his Spanish translation.

After the little boy placed the label DRDO to the right of the cutout, I requested, "Now read me your seahorse's names."

"This is the English," Toño informed me as he pointed to each sign on the label. "Goldie. This is the Spanish." The child swept his finger under the letters to the right side of the seahorse. "Dr-ado," he read, skipping a vowel.

Sol and I clapped for the second time in ten minutes. Toño perused the remaining origami papers until he found a silver foil square.

"He needs a friend," the little boy commented. Cutting a second seahorse from the metallic paper, Toño pasted the glittering form beside its golden companion. Silently, the smart child made the motions of stretching a rubber band while whispering inaudibly to himself. Leaning over the page of labels, he inscribed SLBA. Toño looked up and smiled broadly. "*Silva*," he announced in perfect dialect. The little boy placed the label above the silver seahorse's tiny head. "Done!" he beamed.

CHAPTER EIGHT

Portraits in Emergent Biliteracy: Blue Turtles and Shocker-Senders

We've covered a lot of ground since we first caught up with our two linguistically rich friends and their construction project in the street outside of Beto's home. In addition to becoming acquainted with the community, meeting the boys' families, and wandering the halls of Mariposa Elementary School, we've visited the Science Park and local library where the boys showcased their emergent biliterate proficiencies after a nine-month period. Yet, we still need to synthesize what Toño and Beto's case studies can teach us about the larger process of emergent biliteracy.

Let's return to the boys. We can borrow their bikes and take a spin around the block while we consider the evidence from each microgenetic account. Talking about talking and thinking about thinking is hard work, so we might as well enjoy ourselves. Hop on and let's get going!

Characteristics of Emergent Biliteracy Acquisition

The initial motivation for our study was to identify what semiotic or meaning making means students like Toño and Beto use to make sense of the world when acquiring the processes of listening, speaking, reading, and writing in two languages. The children and their families have taught us that, contrary to deficit views about children and bilingualism in our society, emergent biliteracy is a complex, vibrant, and sophisticated psycho-sociolinguistic process. Our emergent biliterates tapped a conglomerate of biological, familial, cultural and institutional resources when developing dual language and literacy proficiencies. These sources especially included intellectual and emotional capital from informal and formal learning contexts that positively resonated with the boys' growing sense of humor, worth, and self. If we look at Beto and Toño's examples very closely, what do we see?

A Distinct Form of Semiotic Development

Historically, we have viewed bilinguals in dichotomous terms. We have imagined that young children make meaning in one sign system and then "translate" their knowledge into a second code. Or we have assumed that the bilingual mind is composed of two distinct linguistic halves that add up to a communicative whole. Both these binary perspectives are incorrect. The boys' case studies depict emergent biliteracy as a distinct form of meaning making, involving a larger mastery of sign and speech form *in two languages*. In other words, biliteracy development is another beast: Given the appropriate conditions, it is qualitatively distinguished from the process of second-language acquisition.

Emergent bilinguals like Beto and Toño unconsciously acquire the oral and pragmatic features of the dual-language communities into which they are socialized. The development of biliterate proficiencies is not just a simple matter of translating one language into the other or two languages from oral into written form. While oral and written language share common characteristics, including syntax, grammar, and vocabulary, their *psychological functions* remain distinct.

Like their monolingual peers, emergent biliterates like Toño and Beto must also develop a distinction between the dialogical or conversational forms of oral speech and the monologic functions of inner and written speech for Spanish and English. This complicated task involves the extended mastery of signs of two languages in meaning-making situations. Phonemic aspects of the first language's sound system will carry to the second language. As we saw with Toño's fish tale, once acquired, sound can be written in either code.

A Highly Individualized Process

Beto and Toño's portraits strongly portray that the initial acquisition of biliterate means is a highly individualized process. In lieu of the hierarchical stages and vertical standards promoted by various psychologies, professional organizations, and political institutions, our microgenetic evidence confirms that children of the same age, gender, family structure, culture, community, ethnic heritage, linguistic tradition, socioeconomic status, and educational experiences exhibit diverse routes to biliterate acquisition. The children's developmental trajectories or ontogeneses reveal two quantitative, qualitative, and transformationally distinct accounts.

For example, Toño progressed through three transformational phases between the months of December and August. If we were drawing a visual representation of Toño's biliteracy acquisition, it would be characterized by a series of vertical integrations across various listening, speaking, reading, and writing proficiencies. The child demonstrated only a passing interest in books, preferring to write when presented with the opportunity to listen to a read-aloud. In hindsight, Toño actually backed into reading through the writing process. His oral development of Spanish emerged during the summer months. At the end of eight months, Toño employed several emergent biliteracy practices in both Spanish and English.

On the other hand, Beto's emergent biliteracy acquisition was also marked by three transformational phases. However, his ontogenesis involved a foundational period lasting three months. This essential interval was followed by tri-linear and wholistic transformations, for the duration of a month and a half. Qualitatively, Beto's emergent biliteracy acquisition initially involved the mindful, circular exploration, appropriation, and application of listening, speaking, and reading proficiencies in two languages. If we were to visually represent his individual process, we would use a large, repetitive circle that eventually subsumed into a spiral. Once the little boy established a foundation of understanding regarding signs and texts, Beto advanced joyfully into the writing process. In contrast to his peer, Beto's oral development in English emerged *prior to his development of written sign* in the mid-spring. At the end of eight months, Beto also demonstrated several emergent biliteracy practices in English and Spanish. His proficiencies were different yet equitable to the practices of his *compañero*.

From a Vygotskian perspective, this finding validates the diversity of lived experience, funds of knowledge, and cognitive pluralism that constitute *all* of our learning and development. Beto and Toño brought their own unique socio-biological, cultural-historical, and socio-political potentials to the acquisition table. The collective histories of their families coupled with the boys' personal induction into the formal education system provided, and sometimes denied, access to zones of proximal development, impacting their ontological growth. At the same time, Beto and Toño's perezhivanija were sculpted by the children's own preferences, choices, attitudes, and behaviors. Indeed, the final library accounts reflect that the boys' personal amusements and individual sense of humor played a significant role in their biliteracy development. Like a kaleidoscope with multiple visual elements, each boy's microgenesis organized, revolved, and reframed common and distinct components, creating a wholly unique form of biliteracy in the hands of the children's own significance and agency.

The Use of Multiple Resources for Meaning Making

Another key understanding derived from the boys' biliteracy development affirms the creative, resourceful practices of young children and biliterate individuals. In several instances, both Toño and Beto used the structural, functional, or pragmatic features of their two languages as resources for meaning making. A simultaneous bilingual, Toño started school with English vocabulary, syntax, and grammar as his dominant language. At the same time, to a smaller degree, he employed the linguistic structures of Spanish as his less developed language. In contrast, as a sequential bilingual, Beto demonstrated a strong foundation in Spanish as his dominant language. He required the context of school and our experiential sessions together to access the subsystems of English as his less dominant language.

Beto and Toño acquired their less developed oral languages unconsciously (Vygotsky, 1987). The boys' emerging oral speech proficiencies in both languages were developed, enhanced, and refined from the need to make meaning with their age mates and teacher. This semiotic requisite fueled and sustained even the most limited exchanges between the children, their friends, and their adult caregivers. As a result, Beto and Toño's initial oral language functions developed in a spontaneous, involuntary, and informal manner, often as a supplementary means to play, instruction, or action. In other words, they learned their languages by living through them. For the most part, the boys' emergent listening and speaking proficiencies were unconscious to the children, unless events directly elicited their proficiencies in a spontaneous or automatic manner.

Beto's Linguistic Ingenuity. For example, Beto's retort to Patrick during their dinosaur play provides a good example of the involuntary nature of oral speech. In response to Patrick's challenge, Beto unconsciously resourced structural, functional, and pragmatic features of English presented on television and in the play circle. The little boy also drew on shared knowledge and situational factors, the use of linguistic cues including intonation, pitch, and emphasis, and paralinguistic structures such as body language and gesture to co-construct and relate meaning. Through dialogic participation in the meaning-making process, Beto's dinosaur took on an imaginary adversary while the little boy involuntarily expanded his emerging oral proficiency in his non-dominant language.

A significant aspect of Beto's emergent biliteracy acquisition involved the pragmatic use of oral signs specific to school culture. At the start of kindergarten, Beto was just discovering that aural, visual, kinesthetic, and written signs outside the close-knit circle of his family represented specific meanings. Indeed, his quiet family relied on a great deal of silent, physical signs to communicate intent. Facial expressions, physical touch, and indicatory motions signified lived experience between the *chapito* and his relatives. In Beto's tight-knit, home life, the physical presence of objects, entities, and individuals reduced the need for overt, extended discussion, descriptive accounts, or elaborated storytelling.

Beto relied on these first-order, pragmatic features of Spanish as a meaning-making resource while acquiring emergent oral proficiencies in English. His heightened abilities to interpret his physical surroundings, behavioral situations, and the intentions of other individuals sustained his initial acquisition of academic language in Spanish and English. After a four-and-a-half-month period of relative silence in *both* his languages, Beto emerged with a sophisticated command of English syntax. In contrast to cumulative stage theories, Beto swung from complete silence to conversations hallmarked by full sentences and the proper use of contractions and indirect objects. During this time, his emergent oral language expanded to include academic vocabulary, rhymes, and chants in both languages.

Further, Beto's oral speech emergence was not limited to the use of Spanish or English signs in direct communication. He employed the structural, functional, and pragmatic features of *both* his languages to translate and selectively code-switch as a means to solve covert problems among his friends. The little boy showed great facility for discourse/register shifts during play and formal speech events. With a superior, pragmatic foundation in both languages, Beto eventually served as a bilingual mediator for his classmates. This activity further enhanced his acquisition, fluency, and social status.

Toño's Creative Lexical Structures. It was also necessary for Toño to appropriate novel aspects of pragmatic language use in order to develop his emerging biliterate proficiencies: In time, his tantrums were significantly reduced and replaced by the sociocultural norms of his new speech community in our kindergarten.

Acquiring more conventional social language proficiencies widened his circle of friends; the little boy's desire for friendship motivated him to develop the interpersonal patterns, intrapersonal patience, and temporary suspension of certainty that underlie emerging biliteracy development.

Toño's listening and speaking proficiencies in Spanish emerged across an eight-month period. In December, his oral expression was limited to a choice handful of expletives, although he understood much more Spanish. By the end of the summer, Toño could engage in basic conversations with a small lexicon of words. Like his *compañero* Beto, the little boy exhibited the ability to code-switch with single words like *pez* (fish) and *baño* (bathroom). His eagerness to translate aspects of Beto's speech at the seal and polar bear exhibits reflected Toño's desire to communicate with Spanish speakers, conduct basic conversations, read context, and predict meanings he could not already interpret.

As his profile attests, Toño resourced the structural, functional, and pragmatic features of his two languages to make meaning in several ways. He employed his emerging phonemic and morphological knowledge of Spanish to invent words, names, and chants. During the construction of his fish collage, linguistic approximations, including "Golda" for "Goldie" or "Silva" for a female silver seahorse, demonstrated the knowledgeable application of aspects of Spanish signs.

In a final note, Toño's oral language proficiencies offer us an interesting finding regarding his use of words or verbal signs as meaning-making categories. When the child could not produce a term to express his communicative intent in Spanish *or* English, Toño applied one of two linguistic strategies: In the first approach, the little boy combined verbal, kinesthetic, and aural gestures to act out exactly to that which he was referring. Toño's role-play of the motor boat illustrated his use of this strategy.

However, as the little boy's oral lexicon or vocabulary became more enhanced in both languages, Toño adopted a second meaning-making strategy into his linguistic repertoire. When the little boy did not know the name for a specific verbal sign, Toño would invent a novel term, relating meaningful descriptive or functional features of the object, individual, or phenomenon. An example of this strategy occurred when Toño generated the word "carpet-spanker" for "hanger" early in the summer. Our trip to the Science Park yielded a plethora of lexical categories of this nature. Toño invented an especially extensive collection of names during our aquarium visit. His list of sea creatures constituted over twelve names including "shocker-senders" for jelly fish. These creative linguistic strategies supported the child's attempts at meaning making while developing everyday and academic vocabulary in two languages. Subsequent research on Toño's strategy with additional children might shed light on the creative nature of linguistically rich or biliterate individuals.

First- and Second-Order Sign Development Across Codes and Contexts

How did Beto and Toño develop writing? Vygotsky (1978) advised us that, for the monolingual child, written speech is "the culmination of a long process of development of complex behavioral functions in the child" (Vygotsky, 1978, p. 106). The boys' semiotic portraits portray the measured but active shift from what Vygotsky called the first-order symbols of speech to the second-order signs of written language across codes and contexts. What did this transition look like for our two emergent biliterates?

Receptive Knowledge of Written Signs for Productive Development

Parents, teachers, and psychologists have long observed that writing develops only after oral speech and play are well established (Vygotsky (1978; 1997). As emergent biliterates, Beto and Toño's case studies further confirm that knowledge of the receptive aspect of written signs is essential for writing to emerge in two languages.

Toño's receptive knowledge of written signs. Toño acquired written speech after he possessed a solid foundation in text knowledge and book handling practices. His prior experiences with books, magazines, newspapers, cartoons, and other literate genres supported a general understanding of the function of written signs and texts. A review of Toño's written sign acquisition notes a predominance of English over Spanish letters. In December, the child recognized eight out of fifty-four alphabet signs in English. By May, he identified thirty-three out of fifty-four upper- and lowercase letters and produced sounds for sixteen signs in his dominant language. At the same time, Toño could also articulate five letter sounds in Spanish. It is probable the child's repertoire of Spanish signs would have been much more extensive if Toño's inconsistent attendance had not restricted his opportunities for instruction, peer modeling, and scaffolded reading events. It is also possible his receptive knowledge of Spanish signs was greater than the testing situation elicited.

In May, Toño also had a strong understanding of the receptive properties of pictographic speech or visual symbols. He applied picture cues to predict words and interpret logical outcomes for stories. At the Science Park, the young boy displayed emergent reading proficiencies by establishing meaningful connections between oral and graphic signs of the map he was reading. With a minimal amount of explanation, Toño learned that the animal icons on his map identified which creatures lived in the various exhibits as well as their approximate relationship to his own physical location. A revolution occurred in Toño's receptive sign use when the child discovered the ability to symbol-read for informational, geographic, and organizational purposes. This revelation freed him from his present circumstances and allowed him to manipulate his sister: The little boy's ability to logo-read resulted in Sol's purchase of a toy at the gift store. Toño's strengths in reading environmental print, logos, pictographic and ideographic speech girded the productive use of his emergent writing in his drawings and journals.

Beto's receptive knowledge of written signs. In contrast, Beto did not have as an extensive history of interactions or knowledge of the receptive dimension of written signs. In December, the young boy demonstrated an unfamiliarity with printed materials, writing utensils, numbers, and the alphabet. Beto's emerging book knowledge and handling skills were very slowly acquired through informal, formal, and peer modeling from winter through early spring. After receiving direct and scaffolded instruction, the child learned to use pictographic and ideographic speech signs on and in texts to establish positionality, finger tracking, picture reading, prediction, and plot confirmation.

In late spring, Beto developed an emergent understanding of the receptive aspect of written signs, drawing a relationship between signs and print, print and sentences, and sentences and oral discourse. After four and a half months of chants, songs, demonstrations, shared and modeled writing, poetry reading, handwriting practice, and other alphabet work, Beto crossed a conceptual bridge and connected the letter F with its corresponding sound. This accomplishment was the first independent match the child made between a random speech sound and its receptive written symbol. Ten days after this revolution, Beto identified sounds for four more alphabet signs. Within a few weeks, the child confirmed the names of ten letters in English and Spanish, matched their upper- and lowercase pairs, and orally produced sounds for six, individual written signs. Beto had discovered the emergent understanding that written signs receptively represent the sounds of speech.

The simultaneous emergence of bilingual speech, grapho-linguistic relationships, and knowledge of narrative structure motivated the little boy to read independently during self-selection time for the first time in early May. Beto set his cars aside and explored a favorite book we had previously read together. The child accessed each page and its text without assistance. Using the illustrations as cues, Beto whispered an approximation of the plot while identifying letter names and sounds he proudly recognized. In a process similar to his oral language development, Beto required a nesting period to construct an emergent understanding of the receptive aspect of pictographic and ideographic signs. It is significant to note Beto's development of written speech did not commence until he had acquired fundamental verbal and emergent reading proficiencies in both languages.

The Distinction of Speech Forms

An aspect in the boys' development of first- (oral) and second- (written) order sign systems in Spanish and English included the distinction of speech forms. While written signs designate meanings originally represented in oral language, the process of learning to write required the boys to develop and employ a level of abstract thought that "is constructed over and rises above oral speech" (Vygotsky, 1987, p. 203).

This psychological requisite is due to the fact that written speech is a qualitatively different form than its oral predecessor. Beto and Toño's written speech developed differently than their oral language due to its unique structure, function, and level of cognition (Vygotsky, 1987). Indeed, the abstract nature of writing presented difficulties for Beto and Toño alike. In struggling to develop written speech, young writers are challenged by the mute, soundless nature of meaning making and the absence of a visible conversant or audience. It is no coincidence that Toño began to produce a large amount of writing after I stationed a post office with an authentic mailbox in our classroom. The little boy immediately began to construct a plethora of artifacts knowing an attentive recipient would serve as an interested audience for his meaning-making.

Vygotsky (1987) also noted written speech remains an elusive and nebulous concept for young children if they do not have some *functional need* for this form of communication. In Beto's case, the child and his mother operated successfully in his world without the benefit of writing. Until the little boy required a system to record the number of times he and his friend won car races, Beto could not see the significance of emergent writing as a psychological tool. The introduction of tally marks was his first use of abstract, written speech signs. Composing books about himself and things he loved as gifts for his family cemented the value of second order signs for Beto.

In developing written speech, all emergent writers ultimately learn that the use of second-order signs is different from talking; writing is dense, specific, wordier, and maximally more expanded than first order symbolism. In dictating stories and journal entries, both Toño and Beto had to consciously abstract verbal speech from one of their two languages to employ "representatives of words rather than words themselves" (Vygotsky, 1987, p. 202). The consciousness and intentionality required for this task facilitated a semiotic reorganization in the meaning-making processes of both boys. Provided with the appropriate context, tools, and time, Beto and Toño were involved in the involuntary and conscious distinction of oral, inner, and written speech forms described in Vygotsky's theory of sign acquisition.

A Correspondence with Vygotsky's Theory of Sign Acquisition

When closely examined, Beto and Toño's microgeneses correspond with a theory of sign development proposed by a youthful Vygotsky. In the seminal work, *Thought and Language*, the young psychologist wrote, "speech development follows the same course and obeys the same laws as the development of all the other mental operations, including the use of signs" (p. 86). However, after describing the Primitive-Natural, Naïve Psychological, External Signs and Operations, and Ingrowth stages, Vygotsky allegedly never referenced his theory again (H. Mahn, personal communication, January 24, 2006).

Instead, the psychologist relied on a more mature, thorough description of written speech found in "The Pre-History of Written Language" in *Mind in Society* and Chapter 7, Volume 4 of *The Collected Works of L.S. Vygotsky* (1997, pp. 131–148). While Vygotsky was interested in issues of bilingualism, his early death prevented him from writing about it. And yet, hidden among the pages of time, Vygotsky's early writing can help us to better understand complex psychological processes including bilingualism, biliteracy, and multimodal communication.

In order to more appropriately characterize Toño and Beto's portraits in emergent biliteracy using Vygotsky's framework, I have renamed his original stages to better capture the sign development of the children. The phases Oral and Gestural Foundations, Initial Mark-Making Processes, Graphic Representations of Descriptive Text, and the Social Construction of Sequential Symbols as Semiotic Signs were adopted to more appropriately reflect the spectrum of first- and second-order sign acquisition by Beto and Toño. Let's take a look at how dual sign acquisition worked for these emergent biliterates of Spanish and English.

Emergent Biliteracy as the Acquisition of Second-Order Symbols in Two Languages

Emergent Biliteracy in the Oral and Gestural Phase

In the first phase of the children's writing development, written speech began as first-order symbolism. Oral language and symbolic play served as the linguistic and conceptual foundations for Beto and Toño's symbolic meaning making: The children's physical gesture, roleplay, and verbal language during this period evidenced writing in its most natural form. Indeed, Vygotsky (1987) considered play a specialized form of speech.

While Toño and Beto enthusiastically engaged in play during self-selection time, the boys' experience in play groups differed greatly. Toño began sessions with peers, only to drift to the side and entertain himself with toys or characters of his own imagination. In contrast, Beto proved to be a consistent and loyal playmate in groups of two to four children. From December through early spring, the little boy relied mostly on gesture and a restricted amount of oral speech in Spanish to communicate his intent. After his verbal emergence in late spring, Beto served as a bilingual mediator for his peers. Interestingly, Toño and Beto's play styles were later replicated through the approaches they assumed in the composition process.

For example, Beto spent a considerable amount of time developing precursors to writing in this Oral-Gestural phase through intensive observation. When his classmates and teacher wrote their names, drew common symbols, and used the physical tools of art and writing, the little boy focused on each activity with mindful precision. Beto abstained from producing independent written signs until mid-spring. However, the little boy's detailed kinesthetic analyses from this phase helped him construct his own physical protocols for writing practices realized in later phases.

Emergent Biliteracy in the Initial Mark-Making Process Phase

During the second phase, the boys' gestural speech of play was extended into mark-making practices. While Toño's written artifacts were advanced beyond this phase in December, the little boy still occasionally exhibited activities from this developmental period when engaged in the writing process. As he composed, Toño actively employed drama, gesture, and self-talk. During the winter and early spring months, it was not unusual for the little boy to sing, dance and talk to the characters he drew on paper. While the child had previously synthesized action and meaning through pencil and mark-making characteristic of this phase, Toño often began drawings with gestural sketches. Toño also recycled fullscale gestural drawings from time to time as noted in his Gestural Horse Drawing and Baseball Cards

A significant feature of writing in the Initial Mark-Making Processes phase involved appropriating the syntax of written sign through the exploration of line, shape, and other visual marks. Like other emergent writers, Toño often identified objects, entities, and events in their mark making after the fact. Vygotsky (1997) described this phase of semiosis as a "representation in embryonic form" (p. 141). With greater control of syntax and subject, Toño's gestural writing and object naming transformed into the intentional use of pictographic speech. In this manner, the evolution of his symbolic thought moved from the end of drawing events to the beginning of the writing experience.

Both Toño and Beto's efforts at letter formation reflected a gradual mastery of the written syntax of alphabetic signs. In December, Toño's name writing practices were characteristic of writers in the Initial Mark-Making Processes phase. The little boy used the edge of the paper as an anchor to position the physical protocol he employed to construct letters. While Toño was able to form the separate signs of his first name, the kinesthetic protocol remained a separate manual activity, unrelated to the intentional spelling of fish names during his collage work from the end of the summer. In the Initial Mark-Making Processes phase, Toño did not comprehend the separate signs he wrote to be representatives of the sounds of his name in oral or external speech. In other words, the physical aspect of Toño's sign use had not met up with the symbolic reason for its existence yet.

During Toño's first transformation, the child began to break out of name writing as a kinesthetic, whole-word protocol to encode his nickname. This qualitative shift allowed for continued mastery of the external structure of sign and simple mark making. With time, Toño adopted appropriate written conventions including directionality, page placement, and sign reversals and began to represent his last name. His efforts at name writing reflected an increasing appropriation of the syntax of signs.

The development of Beto's written signature followed a parallel course. By observing his age mates and teacher practice handwriting strokes, form letters, construct alphabet signs, and affix signatures, the child received the visual modeling necessary to appropriate the written signs in his own name. With support and encouragement, Beto was able to write the correct letters in his first name by mid-January. Like his *compañero*, Beto's understanding of the specific signs was limited to a kinesthetic protocol of marks he was told represented his name.

While Toño's mastery of alphabetic signs was eventually assumed into the larger process of his biliteracy acquisition, the evolution of Beto's signature involved the development of formal notions regarding literacy. In appropriating his name, Beto learned the art of sign formation, sequencing, and convention. His "one word literacy" paralleled Beto's acquisition of larger concepts specific to the books we read on a larger scale. In struggling to correctly formulate the abstract signs in his name, Beto also acquired notions regarding concepts of print, directionality, spacing, letters vs. initials, and words as opposed to print.

Beto's growing sense of written sign began to emerge during his first transformation. Toward the end of February, he independently formed an upper- and lower-case letter and sound for the signs Bb, Cc, and Dd. At the start of the Initial Mark-Making Processes phase, these signs first appeared as a jumble of random lines and shapes to the boy. By the end of this phase, he could identify the signs and sounds in a manner reflective of Vygotsky's (1987) object drawings. Beto did not associate the abstract sounds of speech with ideographic print until he transitioned from the physical representation of isolated signs in his first and last name to writing his full signature as a meaningful symbol in early March.

This shift hallmarked a significant feature of writing development in Beto's Initial Mark-Making Processes period. Vygotsky (1978) describes this revolution for us as "not something self-understood and purely mechanical. There is a critical moment in going from simple mark-making on paper to the use of pencil marks as signs that depict or mean something" (p. 113). Beto's discovery that he could signify his name using graphic speech hallmarked an important moment in his writing development and meaning making as a whole.

In considering Beto's earliest artifact of pictographic speech, the drawing of his father from December exhibited a primitive, elemental use of shape characteristic of the Initial Mark-Making Processes phase. It is important to note that it was not until mid-spring that Beto independently engaged in the construction of visual imagery or figurative speech to express his ideas.

The opportunity to illustrate his book, *The Two Friends/Los dos amigos*, launched Beto into the creation of pictographic speech characteristic of the Initial Mark-Making Processes phase. The task required the boy to depict himself using graphic speech. The simplistic line of his kingly portrait evidenced his continued mastery of the external structure of sign and syntax in pictograph writing.

Most notably, Beto's read-aloud of, *The Two Friends/Los dos amigos*, signaled the start of a new phase in his writing development. The ability to compose and share a self-story with the assistance of an adult proved to be one of the strongest influences on Beto's emergent biliteracy acquisition. The opportunity to co-write a text about himself and his friend in a playful context literally and figuratively placed both boys into the world of books. The act of using their own words in Spanish and English defined Beto and his *amiguito* as characters and writers of their own story. The power of seeing one's reflection in name, illustration, and plot transformed the meaning of the multilingual world of signs, print, and books for Beto. Aside from adding a playful and validating experience, the public appreciation of Beto's emergent reading and writing proficiencies advanced his status as an emergent biliterate among his classmates.

Emergent Biliteracy and the Graphic Representation of Descriptive Text Phase

The unique and diverse character of the boys' written speech development was especially observed during the period in which Toño and Beto engaged in the third phase. During the interval in the Graphic Representation of Descriptive Text, the young writers abandoned the post-hoc discovery of objects or entities in their drawings to purposely depict pre-planned visual signs. The integration of communicative intent and design fundamentals in Toño's drawings indicated the child had already progressed into this phase in early December. Stick figures from his first Family Portrait suggested that he had previously appropriated and recycled fundamental mark-making practices typical of the Initial Mark-Making Processes phase from siblings, relatives, or more advanced peers.

In contrast, Toño's Self Portrait and Second Family Portrait were distinguished by the introduction of color and contour line. These modifications highlighted a shift from simple marks to the pre-planned representation of complex signs. Exaggerated properties of color, line, shape, and size provided an enhanced visual syntax relating graphic speech. Toño's transition from suggestive to figurative forms allowed for a greater depth of descriptive meanings about his family members in these first-order signs. Through his graphic speech, Toño resembled "only the essential and constant characteristics of objects" or entities significant to him (Vygotsky, 1997, p. 138). In reviewing the child's drawings, we see why Vygotsky compared object drawings produced during this third phase to the naming process exhibited by three-and four-year- olds.

Further analysis of Toño's Self Portrait suggested the child progressed through several phases of sign development during the execution of the single drawing. Toño began the compositional process using drama, cryptic self-talk, and active gestures characteristic of the Oral and Gestural Foundations phase. He initially depicted his torso and head with a gestural cross and circle, also suggestive of indicatory mark making from the same period. However, the elaboration of his figure, sun, and clouds through the intentional depiction of shape and color reflected the phase of the Graphic Representation of Descriptive Text. Toño's portrait presented a full-fledged depiction of himself outside on a cloudy day.

Toño's first Man-Eating Sea Creature Drawing provided the best example of the little boy's pictographic writing from the Graphic Representation of Descriptive Text phase. This drawing also marked Toño's transformation from simple figurative sign use to the complex depiction of narrative accounts.

While his previous writing presented gestural sketches or object drawings, Toño's epic account portrayed two characters and a plot based on cause and effect. The child's conscious selection and intentional record of graphic speech related a dangerous tale of life and death through visual language. Due to the sophisticated content of the story, it is not surprising Toño rapidly advanced towards the appropriation of more efficient mediational means to record his colorful narratives.

In contrast, Beto vacillated between the Initial Mark-Making Processes and Graphic Representation of Descriptive Text phases with scaffolded assistance. The publication of, *The Horses/Los caballos*, required the child to produce a sign he personally did not know how to construct. After I modeled and scaffolded how to draw a horse from shapes I knew the child could produce, Beto repeatedly practiced the visual sign until he could independently depict the graphic image by himself. The little boy successfully completed an illustration for one of the pages of his book, feeling a rush of pride regarding his accomplishment.

After this exchange, the little boy frequently asked me to demonstrate how to configure pictographic speech of his interest. In the classroom, we retained a small plastic bag filled with index cards of the visual signs I modeled and helped him to depict. During journal time, Beto referenced his bag of signs for independent writing when he and I were not adding a new picture to the collection. His First Letter proved to be a significant artifact from this phase in that the horse and worm signs Beto depicted were produced from the child's memory at home. Modeling, scaffolding, and praise propelled Beto toward an intentional use of graphic speech while enriching a growing lexicon of visual vocabulary.

The most significant visual sign in Beto's collection of graphic words was the symbol of the *tortuga azúl* or blue turtle. Once the child learned how to represent his favorite creature, the blue turtle became a motif in all of Beto's drawings, dictations, journals, and books. The little boy requested literary artifacts including books, films, and magazines about turtles during the spring and the summer. Beto's fascination with turtles was reflected in the bookmaking activity related in the representative account that occurred after our trip to the Science Park.

At first, the child was uncertain about his role in writing, *The Adventures of Superheroes Beto and Tere/Las adventuras de superheroes Beto and Tere*. With prompting, linguistic scaffolding, and conceptual echoing, ownership for the construction of the book slowly transitioned from me to the young child. Confidence, humor, and encouragement allowed Beto to assume greater ownership in selecting photographs and dictating ideographic speech for both his languages. While the boy was not developmentally ready to independently spell words characteristic of the Ingrowth phase, Vygotsky (1987) viewed Beto's dictation of text as an equivalent and justifiable form of written speech stating, "In writing, he constructs the phrase in the same voluntary and intentional way as he creates the word from separate letters. That is, the child's syntax is as voluntary as his phonetics" (p. 203).

A turning point occurred in our book writing when Beto chose the first snapshot of himself above the turtle exhibit at the Science Park. By placing himself and his love for turtles into the text, Beto re-established himself as a dual character and an author for the second time in a few short months. His comical, repetitive story line to "jump in" and convene with the creatures of his adoration echoed the dream of every child who has ever loved an animal from the opposite side of a fence. Beto's dictated text captured the boy's personality, languages, voice, and sense of humor. The story also indicated his writing had semiotically transformed from the record of everyday reality to the created possibility of fantasy where hopes and dreams are nurtured and born.

In retrospect, the power of the blue turtle sign was so meaningful to the child that Beto continued to write turtle stories two years after our study together was complete. The sign proved to be the "affective hook" that snagged the little boy into written speech, while providing a semiotic vehicle to explore the larger world of biliteracy. Beto's "affective hook" directly related to the child's motivation to become biliterate. Future investigation of these essential metaphors might suggest how to capture and transport young children to literary worlds where their faces, voices, and passions are echoed.

Emergent Biliteracy and the Social Construction of Sequential Symbols as Semiotic Signs

In the final phase of sign acquisition, our boys transitioned from first- to second-order symbolism to the understanding that their own verbal language could be mediated through written signs. While Beto's written development remained at the level of first-order symbolism in the Graphic Representation of Descriptive phase, Toño evidenced this transformation by shifting from pictographic to ideographic writing. This transformation reorganized his biliterate and semiotic proficiencies. Such a dialectical revolution required what Vygotsky (1987) called a "dual abstraction" from the emergent biliterate. In developing written speech, Toño first needed to divorce himself from the auditory aspect of verbal speech usually shared with another in conversation. Second, it was essential for Toño to cultivate a conscious awareness of his own speech abilities, including his developing sense of inner speech, in order to successfully mitigate communicative intent.

To elaborate, Vygotsky asserted that a child's intent is initiated by a motive or an emotion. This affective knowledge becomes manifest in consciousness or thought in the form of internal speech. In order for the word meaning of inner thought to be mediated into second order symbolism, internal speech must transform into verbal thinking, followed by a transitory, unspoken phase as external speech. Instead of being articulated, communicative intent then by-passes oral expression, and is recorded in the written signs of speech. This is why writing is so difficult for monolingual, biliterate, and multilingual individuals alike!

Such a complex procedure involves verbal or external, inner, and written speech functions to record second-order symbols. Therefore, the nature of the writing process requires children, including our boys, to become highly cognizant of these varying forms of speech. For emergent biliterates like Beto, who was still developing proficiencies in two languages, gifts of confidence and time are required to increase vocabulary in two languages while we assist the child in developing a more conscious perception of their speech functions.

During our study, Toño appeared to rely on his dominant language to navigate his development during the phase of Social Construction of Sequential Symbols as Semiotic Signs. Toño's final metamorphosis during the school year was characterized by a synchronicity in aural, kinesthetic, verbal, and written sign use. The integration and involution of these proficiencies produced an explosion in sign development, including the use of "primitive indicatory signs for memory purposes" or mnemotechnic symbols as a hallmark of semiotic internalization (Vygotsky, 1978, p. 115).

For example, Toño's Cartographic Exercise first reflected a shift to simple abstract signs as a primitive form of mnemotechnic symbols. The little boy employed a series of lines and dots to represent city blocks and the number of minutes it took to travel from Toño's doorstep to his classroom. The creation of this simple map signaled a novel form of semiosis where abstract signs were used for memory and calculation purposes.

During the Social Construction of Sequential Symbols as Semiotic Signs phase, Toño, like many children, produced "scribble writing" as a mnemotechnic sign. While the first evidence of scribble words appeared in Toño's journal while his drawings were more reflective of the Initial Mark-making Processes phase, these indicatory lines proved to be precursors for sentences that emerged in later artifacts. During this final phase in sign development, Toño began to incorporate a combination of lines and seminal signs including the first few letters of the alphabet, the numbers 1–8, and uppercase letters from Toño's first name. After conventional signs including hearts, arrows, x's and o's (for hugs and kisses), stars, and dollars and cents symbols had been modeled and interpreted for the class around Valentine's Day, Toño added these cultural symbols to his texts as well. These ideographic signs evidenced the child's emerging relationship between internal speech, verbal thinking, and abstract written symbols.

Toño's appropriation of ideographic signs was also accompanied by an expansion in the number of literary artifacts he produced during his Social Construction of Sequential Symbols as Semiotic Signs phase. His pictographic writing expanded from object and narrative drawings to a multiplicity of written genres including envelopes, newspaper advertisements, valentines, money, and baseball cards all accented by ideographic speech.

Toño's mastery of alphabetic signs in his first, last, and nick names was also at this time. His artifacts revealed a sorting process occurring between upper- and lowercase letters as well as the proper positioning of signs without reversals. Toño's acquisition of the English alphabet was greatly enhanced by chants we sang that coordinated letter names, their sounds, and the movements required to draw each sign in the air. During the early spring, he was able to access an alphabet sign by physically creating its motion. The kinesthetic protocol would be accompanied by the song in his memory. The chant would then lead him to the letter name and its corresponding sound.

Toño relied on these verbal-kinesthetic supports reflective of the Initial Mark-Making Processes phase until the physical scaffolding of the signs became unnecessary during the mid-spring. At that time, Toño remarked, "My brain sings the song to myself!" The internalization of alphabetic signs was additionally evidenced when the little boy encoded his full first and last name in the proper direction, while silently mouthing Spanish phonemes to the syllables. During this final interval, the sounds of several alphabetic signs in English became established in Toño's memory. It is possible, even probable, that the child's receptive knowledge of Spanish signs proved greater than informal tests indicated at the end of the school year.

Several aspects of Toño's drawings from mid-to late spring also located his writing development in the Social Construction of Sequential Symbols as Semiotic Signs phase. The appearance of highly detailed, hieroglyphic-looking signs in Toño's journals represented a form of proto-word, replacing the child's indicatory signs, scribbles, and symbolizing marks from a previous stage. Toño's Mummy Treasure Narrative combined the child's pictographic and ideographic speech. This confluence of visual and written signs was also evidenced in his second drawing of the Man-Eating Sea Creature. In this account, the child's hieroglyphic text is punctuated by the abstract use of line as an index to relate the chronological structure of the visual narrative.

Vygotsky (1978) foreshadowed Toño's writing development when he stated, "Children gradually transform these undifferentiated marks. Indicatory signs and symbolizing marks and scribbles are replaced by little figures and pictures, and these, in turn, give way to signs" (p. 115). Eventually, Toño's wavy scribble writing and hieroglyphics were substituted by strings of letters with long lines underneath them. The little boy's individual letters represented whole words for items advertised in his grocery announcements.Whereas Toño's lines had previously designated plot sequence, in his newspaper announcements, these indices suggested which sign-words were to be collectively read as sentences in speech. The little boy had transitioned from the presentation of objects, entities, and events, to the drawing of words and sentences, employing a host of different types of signs.

Further examination of Toño's microgenesis notes the recycling of gestural line, scribbling, and other primitive design elements from the Initial Mark-Making Processes phase while in his Social Construction of Sequential Symbols as Semiotic Signs phase. At first glance, this phenomenon appeared to be a regression. This belief was entirely incorrect on my part. Hindsight confirmed that Toño's Gestural Horse Drawing and Baseball Cards were actually used as a means to experiment, reorganize, and re-sort sophisticated, ideographic forms that emerged later as intricate alphabet signs. This temporary period in Toño's writing development lends further credence to the notion that children will draw on forms and processes from previous phases of written sign acquisition to support, inform, or advance their current development of emerging forms. The phases of emergent biliteracy acquisition serve as interfunctional supports for children as they develop from first to second-order sign use.

Toño completed the school year as an emergent biliterate who synchronized his own visual, verbal, and written speech. With the assistance of adults, the child recorded the stories, jokes, and chants he invented in English during oral language play. His verbal creations complemented the wide array of literary genres he co-constructed and shared with his friends, family, and teacher. Toño's newfound willingness to dictate journal entries and stories validated Vygotsky's unified process of oral, kinesthetic, graphic, and written speech.

By the end of the school year, Toño understood that the second-order signs of written letters distinctly represented the first order sounds of speech. Further, our conversation regarding his Chinese Calligraphy suggests his understanding extended from Spanish and English to other idioms in his environment. During the late spring, he sought Spanish translations for his texts. However, Toño's Spanish writing emerged during the summer months.

In July, Toño transitioned from the first-order symbolism of dictated speech to independent, second-order sign use in written activity. For the most part, his summer projects retained the graphic speech of the Graphic Representation of Descriptive Text phase. Toño employed a multitude of genres to represent his interest in life underwater, including sculpture, drawing, found- object relief, and collage. While his Seahorse collage retained characteristics of object drawings, Toño's interfunctional, independent use of second-order signs in English and Spanish was launched during the naming process of his aquarium characters.

The christening of Toño's seahorses represented a breakthrough in a variety of ways. In contrast to his letter-word grocery advertisements, Green/Verde, Goldie/Dorado, and Silva were the first full words the child wrote that were constructed from more than one alphabetic sign. Second, after sufficient modeling and scaffolding, Toño assumed independent ownership for representing the individual sounds of speech in written sign. Third, his writing reflected previously emphasized knowledge that many Spanish and English signs share a common phonemic basis. Fourth, while Toño resourced English semantics to name his silver female seahorse, he also independently drew on phonemic and morphological aspects of Spanish to write the namesake "SLBA" or "Silva."

The process of writing the seahorses' names in English and Spanish involved a complicated series of actions involving external, inner and written speech. Toño's intention to name the seahorse moved from motive/emotion to thought in the form of internal speech. Perhaps it was at this point that he decided "Silva" would make a good name. As internal speech, the word "Silva" then transformed into verbal thinking. Toño's verbal thought followed a transitory, unspoken phase as external speech. Instead of being articulated, the term "Silva" by-passed oral expression. Toño then became consciously aware of the word's structure and his own activity in the production of sound. Whispering to himself, he partitioned the word, voluntarily pronouncing each separate sound. As he articulated the Spanish phonemes, Toño recorded the sounds of the word using four random, abstract letter signs he had previously associated as the "S," "L," "B," and "A" sounds. In constructing a written label for Silva, this emergent biliterate transitioned from the first-order symbolism of oral speech to the second-order signs of written language, drawing on strengths from his two codes.

Back to the Boys: A Quick Summary

All in all, Toño and Beto have provided us with two rich accounts and scientific evidence about emergent biliteracy acquisition. Let's take a minute to review what we've been talking about talking and thinking about thinking, derived from their examples.

As a distinct form of semiotic development, we can describe emergent biliteracy as a complex, highly individualized, psycho–sociolinguistic process in which young children utilize multiple resources for meaning making. While evolving from the first-order signs of verbal language to the second-order signs of written speech, children must develop receptive knowledge about writing itself. Emergent biliterates also construct distinctions between various verbal, gestural, pictographic, and written speech forms across a series of texts within multiple contexts. Emergent biliteracy acquisition corresponds with Vygotsky's early Theory of Sign Acquisition. It is hallmarked by an oral and gestural phase, followed by initial mark making processes. After evolving into the graphic representation of descriptive text, emergent biliterates co-construct sequential symbols as semiotic signs appropriate to their use in two distinct speech communities.

Toño's profile especially reflects the creative and linguistic ingenuity of this meaning making process, describing his reality with inventive lexical categories including "shocker-senders." On the other hand, Beto's microgenesis, originating with the symbol of the blue turtle, affirms the causal-dynamic basis of emergent biliteracy rooted in children's need to make meaning *in relationships*. Let's return to the boys and see how they have fared with the bike ramp.

Nurturing Growth: Educational Guidelines to Promote Biliteracy

B eto and Toño's profiles point to a series of educational guidelines we can implement to promote emergent biliteracy for linguistically rich children and their English-dominant peers. Because emergent biliteracy represents a distinct form of meaning making involving the larger psycho-sociolinguistic development, we must refine psychological, pedagogical, and political paradigms. The following strategies are especially meant for fellow educators who seek to nurture the biliterate potential of preschool through second graders in the multilingual school.

Forge Warm, Positive, Trusting Relationships

In order to facilitate biliteracy and intercultural competencies, we must forge warm, positive, trusting relationships with the children entrusted to our care. This paradigm shift is achieved by restructuring the traditional power relationship among teachers and students to that of a caring flow between mentor and novice. It is quite possible Beto would have remained in his silent period for a much longer duration in a more hierarchical classroom. We must respectfully approach our mentees as fellow human beings with the essential need to make meaning through risk-free, joyful, interpersonal communication. Emergent biliterates acquire the sophisticated understandings associated with second- order sign acquisition when we award them the gift of our confidence (Mahn & John-Steiner, 2002) in physical, emotional, linguistic forms.

Teachers of emergent biliterates often "stand in" as temporary mediators for children as they successively appropriate oral and written language. In this capacity, we must honor the messages of our mentees. In order to acquire the semiotic power of their verbal and written speech, mentor-assisted texts need to directly reflect the children's intent as they would write it at a more advanced stage. By ensuring a high correlation between the boys' dictation and their journal statements, Beto and Toño were able to not just know, but *experience* the relationship between and dynamics of verbal and written speech. These perspectives and practices form the basis of trusting relationships for biliteracy acquisition to occur.

Plan for Diversity

Because the biliteracy development is a highly, individualized process, it is important to recognize and respect the diverse evolution of each child. Because the substitute implemented the exact same program for Toño and Beto, several months of precious time were lost, resulting in the retention of the children. Regardless of how or where state, district, or commercial entities standardize our students, children do not, will not, and should not be expected to develop language and literacy proficiencies in a cookie-cutter fashion. While common developmental patterns exist, millions of dollars of research on learning and literacy substantiates this commonsense assertion. Beto and Toño's transformations highlight the diverse nature of language learning. The myth that young children develop in a uniform manner is a throwaway from our industrial age. Interestingly, we have a tendency to apply it only to other people's children. It's time for us to challenge and correct this harmful ideology.

Instead, we need to recognize that our linguistically rich students are language learners in possession of a personal, semiotic inheritance. As Beto and Toño's case studies attest, each boy displayed unique needs and corresponding venues for growth: Toño's visual-verbal style directly contrasted with Beto's auditory-kinesthetic approach. Our journey with the boys across nine months of school dramatically underscores that each child will transform through the stages of emergent biliteracy in a time and manner dictated by their own development. This phenomenon does not mean that we have no responsibility in the matter. On the contrary, we have an even greater responsibility for professional expertise and pedagogical practice. Rather, teachers of emergent biliterates need to expect and plan for a wide range of meaning making styles, entry-level knowledge, attitudes, skills, strategies and behaviors regarding oral and written speech. Young children's cultural familiarity with the physical and psychological tools of school will naturally vary from community to community. The same principle holds for their exposure to and understandings about oral and written signs, print, and texts. Similarly, Beto and Toño's examples validate the kaleidoscope of factors that coalesce and direct the language acquisition process.

In planning for diversity, we provide a balanced, judicious presentation of the two target languages of acquisition. Careful consideration must be made to ensure the even-handed representation and use of both languages with respect to time, tasks, speakers, and materials so the power and potential of each language is equitably realized. This diversity can be achieved through the targeted use of scaffolded supports for auditory-kinesthetic learners like Beto.

Organize Transitions from First- to Second-Order Symbols

In seeking to transition children from first-order to second-order symbol use, Vygotsky (1978) tells us that "The entire secret of teaching written language is to prepare and organize this natural transition appropriately" (p. 115). He insisted that writing be cultivated from children's natural potentialities and preferences rather than imposed from the teacher's initiative. Instead, he encouraged us to organize the actions of gesture, oral language, drawing, and writing to facilitate "the entire complex process of transition from one mode of written language to another" (Vygotsky, 1978, p. 118).

In seeking to organize this psycho-sociolinguistic growth, we can begin by creating a time and space where children are free to engage reading, writing, speaking, and listening in two languages. Beto and Toño developed increasingly sophisticated letter knowledge when signing in each morning. Calendar and weather station activities additionally organized and facilitated conceptual and linguistic growth, combining science and language arts objectives. After observing and collecting multiple samples of children's behavioral, language, and literacy texts, including play sequences, drawings, conversations, and formal tasks, teachers can easily determine each students' current level of sign acquisition. The implementation of a writer's workshop approach in two languages can then be implemented. This process-approach to biliteracy development can be mindfully but flexibly organized to implement an ever-changing array of groups, activities, and interactional formats. By inviting children to employ multimodal means to record their graphic speech such as photographs sculpture and collage, teachers can directly focus on "shifting the children's activity from drawing things to drawing speech" (Vygotsky, 1978, p. 115).

Establish a Print-Rich, Collaborative Environment

In order to facilitate the shift from first-order to second-order signs, a print-rich, collaborative environment must be established as a backdrop. This type of classroom should not be confused with decorating our wall spaces inch by inch with visual "eye candy." In contrast, a print-rich environment functions as a deliberate, visually supportive context. The print-rich environment allows children to exploit physical conditions to read, refer, explore, and utilize written language posted on walls, tables, bookshelves, and in corners. Toño especially enjoyed using our dual English-Spanish word wall when writing independently in his journal.

Print-rich environments actively encourage children to handle a variety of written materials. In this manner, they become familiar with physical and psychological school tools. We can also bring a collection of outside literary artifacts, including church hymnals, food packaging, maps, big books, TV guides, lists, newspapers, and other items to illustrate the receptive dimension of written sign. In print-rich environments, children actively help to maintain the "thinking environment" by cumulatively adding discovered information. For example, Beto and Toño were encouraged to bring in packaging from their favorite foods to add to our word wall. In print-rich environments, emergent biliterates and their teachers contribute to a lexical library to nurture connections between everyday and academic notions about reading and writing.

When establishing a print–rich environment, consider presenting the use of independent signs like the alphabet, numbers, or other written symbols as they exist within larger texts. For example, the boys began to use tally marks when the sign helped to enhance their car play. Beto made deep connections between the numerals that ran across our board when comparing them to produce advertisements. Toño's sign use especially exploded at Valentine's Day when he was able to apply familiar and novel signs in his holiday cards.

This same principle holds for emergent reading proficiencies such as book knowledge and handling skills, concepts of print, prediction, interpretation, and story retelling. These competencies are also fundamental to the writing process. By placing a contextual emphasis on these activities as opposed to presenting them in isolation, emergent biliterates are exposed to *both* the structure and function of narratives they will soon be drawing or writing. I am reminded of a school I once observed who spent so much time drilling kindergartners on letter sounds that read-alouds were absent from the curriculum. How were the children supposed to develop a sense of narrative during which they would apply such signs? In our own classroom, Beto experienced significant growth in book handling skills when we first began our tiny "reading groups." Without the complementary experiences of multilingual story time, shared reading, and literature groups, emergent biliterates will have difficulty developing a sense of the internal structure for written language tapped in the composition process.

The ultimate goal in developing a print-rich, collaborative environment is to mindfully coordinate perezhivanija, or lived experiences, where children actively employ language and literacy for social, cognitive, and academic reasons in two languages. The physical layout of the classroom can be arranged to accommodate whole group, half group, small group, and individual interactions. By deliberately constructing and utilizing a variety of communicative contexts, children's entrance to multiple zones of proximal development is increased, allowing access to authentic language use.

Begin with Play and Extend into Inquiry

Another consideration when organizing children's transition from first- to second-order symbols is for teachers to tap the speech, play, and interests of the children. While this principle appears to be obvious or even considered a luxury by many teachers, very few educators provide more than lip service to this practice. By viewing our students' inquiries, passions, and interests as the basis for instruction, we can motivate and extend the listening, speaking, reading, and writing proficiencies of emergent biliterates in a manner that is powerful and meaningful to the children themselves. Like Beto's first books, educators can introduce a variety of techniques, questions, problem-solving challenges, devices, and/or literary artifacts in the context of play, gently scaffolding children to the use of physical and psychological tools of literacy. The creation of restaurant menus or the labeling and pricing of items in the classroom store present opportunities in which reading and writing in two languages can be integrated into the play circle. The creation of charts, graphs, lists, letters, and other messages for play sequences locates sign, print, and text inside children's imaginative worlds. Like our snowflake report, by composing and publishing drawings, stories, poems, journals, and chants about the content of children's play, emergent biliterates are dynamically placed *into* the world of sign, print, and text.

Play sequences also offer us teachable moments where we can address children's questions raised during formal instruction. These curiosities can be reflected back to the play circle while being used as thematic inquiries for engaged research. Committees can investigate topics from content areas, as we did with our weather station, while role-play provides the the opportunity to process the meanings they discover in two languages. Intensive development occurs across languages when we present and support linguistically rich students with the challenge of investigating a mystery, solving a problem, or discovering a fascinating aspect of their interest.

Honor Children's Lives

In order for young children to acquire biliterate proficiencies, they must be engaged in authentic activities that are intrinsically necessary, meaningful, and relevant to their school *and home* lives. Like Beto's framed turtle picture and Toño's baseball cards, the gift of a book, a song commemorating a birthday, or an invitation to a Pooh party all include biliterate means that bridge home and school. As teachers, we can help shape the selection and execution of such projects by honoring the necessary, meaningful, and relevant in our students' lives, harnessing meaningful reasons to speak, listen, read, and write in two languages.

Allow Sufficient Time for Development

It is also important for us to remember that children need time, patience, and sufficient engagement to distinguish between the dialogical forms of oral language and monological functions of inner and written speech. As we witnessed with Beto and Toño, an extensive amount of preparation was required for the complex, early acquisition of written signs. Because emergent biliteracy is partially dependent on the mastery of oral language, as well as our modeling and scaffolding as mentors, development requires sufficient time. As both the boys' case studies suggest, emergent biliterates will draw on forms and activities from previous stages of sign development to support, inform, or advance their current use of sign. Therefore, young children need time each day to consider, construct, experiment, invent, explore, and/or otherwise engage with written language. To the untrained eye, this practice might appear to be a waste of instructional minutes. However, from a psycholinguistic perspective, literacy activities during self-selection time encompass a host of sophisticated practices, cultivating reading, writing, speaking and listening as well as problem-solving and creativity. In short, it is essential for us to schedule and commit to observing a consistent writing time on a daily basis. Our confidence, patience, and time are necessary requirements for children like Toño and Beto to develop second-order symbol systems and a sophisticated sense of the monologic forms of speech.

Focus on Generative, Joint Productive Activity

During the writing hour, we can best focus on the construction of texts through collaboration or joint productive activity. Emergent biliterates and their teachers can write by themselves, or in dyads, triads, or teacher/mentor assisted groups. All children need to be engaged in the production of a written artifact of their own selection or creation. In an ideal situation, emergent biliterates involved in small group activities or other collective efforts would still have a chance to write in a journal sometime during day.

Children's efforts at acquiring written speech are sustained by their own vivid imaginations. Toño's creation of artifacts from multiple genres begs for us to reconsider the role of coloring books, number-to-dot drawings, or other pre-printed commercial signs we include in our classrooms with the best of all intentions. While media imagery will appear in children's writing from time to time, emergent biliterates can be directed to develop their own lexicon of pictographic and ideographic speech. Such encouragement, in the long run, nurtures the voice of the writer and their subsequent narratives. Even a small amount of joint productive activity promotes the creation of a wide range of artifacts that put electronic media to shame. Through assisted problem solving, children's poetry, drama, artwork, and writing reflect a sophistication and richness that readily surpasses the shallow hype of high-tech imagery or print.

Interestingly, for Beto and other emergent biliterates, it is not enough to learn that letters represent speech sounds; the little boy had to learn that his *own speech sounds* could be represented by alphabetic signs. By engaging in the co-creation of autobiographical stories about himself, the emergent biliterate was placed in a dual role as the main character *and* writer. Writing self-narratives in a collaborative manner helped Beto to establish the abstract connection between sign and speech. Using a child's words in two languages validates the potential of their emergent biliteracy, especially when linguistically rich children witness their own name, imagery, and selves as they appear in the plot. Inner speech becomes linked with the external print of the text. When appropriately trained, paraprofessionals, parents, volunteers, high school tutors, grandparents, and other advanced peers can assist teachers in producing and publishing student work.

Model and Scaffold a Host of Writing Genres

Because our mentees' written language acquisition relies on the example and expertise of more advanced writers, it is important that we model and scaffold a host of writing events for emergent biliterates. Vygotsky (1987) reminds us that "Instruction depends on processes that have not yet matured, processes that have just entered the first phases of their development" (p. 205). Our role as educators is to seize the opportunity of youth and make the hidden aspects of inner and written speech forms explicit in both languages. Sharing the pen with our students illuminates the often indiscernable nature of the writing process. Teachers can make the invisible visible for children in all phases of biliteracy development through modeled, shared, guided, and assisted writing formats.

In our class, Toño and Beto became conscious of oral, inner, and written speech forms through regular write-alouds where I related the thought processes behind my own choice making. Modeling provides children with an actual example of physical or psychological tool use. Teachers can also exploit peer modeling by strategically pairing specific children together. Scaffolding occurs when we assist emergent biliterates by recording their written speech through physical, conceptual, affective, and other devices. Toño's fish collage is a good example of a text with a variety of these multimodal means. Educators can support novice writers by questioning, echoing, substitutions, spotlighting, and mirroring as means to call the emergent biliterate's attention to the intentionality and specific features of written speech in two distinct languages.

Talk about the Process

As we assist our mentees' transition from first-order signs to second-order symbolism in two languages, we can talk about the process of becoming biliterate with individual students and our classes. During writing time, educators need to ask both what a child's drawing/writing means and how they captured their speech on paper. With prompting, students can discuss their work with peers, highlighting the explicit means used to construct a drawing or story. Toño especially loved to share why and *how* he came up with his own onomatopoeic raps. With scaffolding, his peers provided feedback on their *amiguitos'* work, thereby promoting Toño's conscious control of syntax and subject. Through group discussion, examples, and praise, linguistically rich children can enrich their emerging graphic and written lexicons while moving toward the intentional use of written speech.

The challenge is for teachers to discuss the conditions of biliteracy acquisition with young children in a manner that is meaningful to them. The boys and I employed several metaphors to help us discuss the nature of the writing process. Because the acquisition of biliterate proficiencies is intimately tied to a growing sense of identity, competence, and value, praising the emergent biliterate's talents, efforts, and abilities at translation, code-switching, intercultural competencies, discourse shift, and the use of extra-linguistic cues is paramount. In helping to cultivate the psychological "voice" engaged in meaning-making, we need to build resilience against the frustration, uncertainty, and sense of isolation that sometimes characterizes biliteracy acquisition.

Conversations with children about specific strategies, including the rubber band method of sounding out words, helps emergent biliterates to develop fluency. Young children are always eager to share how they solve problems with friends regardless of the challenge. Whether their concerns involve structural, functional, or pragmatic features of sign use or communication failure, children devise the most wonderful solutions when asked to assist a peer. By talking about the acquisition processes, we can help make the unique behaviors that characterize the dual language experience more explicit, strengthing and giving credence to the designation "linguistically rich."

Celebrate Successive Approximations and Mini-Victories

Because parts of our society have become increasingly hostile toward bilingualism, it is necessary to develop the resilience of our mentees by presenting its many cognitive, affective, social, political, and occupational benefits. We can highlight the merits of bilingualism to counter incorrect and harmful social messages that often silence young linguistically rich children. Fortunately, the nature of our work presents multiple, daily opportunities to celebrate the successive approximations and mini-victories displayed in the process of becoming biliterate. Teachers can recruit a larger audience of adults to praise children's emerging proficiencies in a variety of ways, from forwarding positive notes home to providing public recognition at school assemblies. After recruiting a friendly secretary in the front office for this very purpose, Toño and Beto beamed with pride after hearing the impact their valentine cards had on my colleague's day. Children need to know that the power of their words matters. Experiencing recognition, praise, encouragement, and approval from family and community members can sustain or inspire children who might be struggling with the absence of biliterate role models. Indeed, the intersection of need, function, and audience will often motivate and sustain emergent biliterates like Beto and Toño in the development of two written languages.

Wall Builders, Gate Keepers, or Rampbuilders?

While many of the suggested guidelines from this chapter can be easily and effectively implemented, we need to bear in mind that the larger process of biliteracy acquisition transcends beyond the mastery of first- and second-order signs in dual-language systems. Vygotsky (1962) advises us that children's "thought must be known, but not as the enemy must be known in order to be thought successfully" (p. 86). In the end, this complex, psycho-sociolinguistic process is all about voice, identity, and meaning making among human beings.

In order to support and nurture emergent biliterates, a fundamental condition must be present: we must reach out to respect, care, and educate *all* linguistically rich children regardless of "race"/ethnicity, class, gender, religion, ability, or language. Without happy, healthy, and safe relationships, administrators and teachers will continue to physically, literally, and figuratively construct "language barriers," placing the educational backs of young children, their families, and their communities against the wall.

Indeed, as we catch up with Beto and Toño, we see these creative, innovative children, like millions of their peers, have all it takes to expertly bike around on the wheels of two languages when given the chance. As the boys take turns with their newly constructed jump, their shouts in two languages echo across the rooftops. It is time for us to imagine this same scenario replicated across a nation of neighborhoods. Within this global, multilingual, technological age, it is *our responsibility* to roll up our sleeves, get close to the ground, and build the academic ramps that allow *all children* the opportunity to defy gravity and fly. If we do so, the sparkling joy of laughter will trail these young, biliterate Americans as they bounce proudly into the future waiting just down the street.

References

August, D., and Shanahan, T. (2006). (Eds). *Developing literacy in second-language learners: report of the National Literacy Panel on language-minority children and youth.* Mahwah, NJ: Lawrence Earlbaum.

Axline, V. (1967). *Dibs in search of self.* New York: Ballantine Books.

Baca, L., and Cervantes, H. (2004). *The bilingual special education interface.* (4th ed.). Upper Saddle River, NJ: Pearson Education, Inc.

Baker, C. (2001). *Foundations of bilingual education and bilingualism.* (3rd ed). Tonawanda, NY: Multilingual Matters. Ltd.

Bruner, J. (1990). *Acts of meaning.* Cambridge: Harvard University Press.

Bruner, J. (1983). *Child's talk:Learning to use language.* New York: Norton & Company.

Christian, D. (2006). Introduction. In Genessee, et al., *Educating English language learners: a synthesis of research evidence* (pp. 1–11). New York: Cambridge University Press.

Cole, M. (1996). *Cultural psychology: A once and future discipline.* Cambridge, MA: Harvard University Press.

Cole, M. (1990). Cognitive development and formal schooling: The evidence from cross-cultural research. In L.C. Moll (Ed.) *Vygotsky and education: Instructional implications and applications of sociohistorical psychology.* (pp. 89–110). Cambridge: Cambridge University Press.

Collier, V.P. (1987). Age and rate of acquisition of second language for academic purposes. *TESOL Quarterly*, Volume 21, Number 4, pp. 617–641.

Crawford, J. (2004). *Educating English learners: Language diversity in the classroom.* (5th ed.) Los Angeles, CA: Bilingual Education Services.

Cummins, J. (1981). The role of primary language development in promoting educational success for language minority students. In California State Department of Education, *Schooling and language minority students: A theoretical framework.* (pp. 3–49). Los Angeles: California State University; Evaluation, Dissemination, and Assessment Center.

De la Luz-Reyes, M., (2001). Unleasing possibilities: biliteracy in the primary grades. In de la Luz-Reyes and Halcón, (Eds.) *The best for our children: Critical perspectives on literacy for Latino students* (pp. 96–121). New York: Teachers College Press.

Denzin, N. K., and Lincoln, Y.S. (Eds.). (2000). *Handbook of qualitative research.* (2nd ed.) Thousand Oaks, CA: Sage Publications.

Echevarria, J., Vogt, M., and Short, D. (2004). *Making content comprehensible for English learners: the SIOP model.* (2nd ed.) Boston: Pearson.

Echiburu-Berzins, M., and Lopez, A.E. (2001). Starting off right: planting the seeds for biliteracy. In de la Luz-Reyes and Halcón (Eds.). *The best for our children: Critical perspectives on literacy for Latino students* (pp. 81–95). New York: Teachers College Press.

Faltis, C. (2006). *Teaching English-language learners in elementary school communities: A joinfostering approach.* Uppersaddle River, NJ: Pearson Prentice-Hall.

Gardner, H. (1993). *Frames of mind: The theory of multiple intelligences.* New York: Basic Books, Inc.

Genesee, F., Lindholm-Leary, K., Saunders, W., and Christian, D. (2006). *Educating English language learners: A synthesis of research evidence.* New York: Cambridge University Press.

Genesee, F., and Riches, C. (2006). Instructional Issues. In Genessee, et al., *Educating English language learners: A synthesis of research evidence* (pp. 109–143). New York: Cambridge University Press.

Goldenberg, C. (2008). Teaching English language learners: what the research does and does not say. *American Educator,* Summer, pp. 8–44, 2008.

Goodman, K., Goodman, Y., and Flores, B. (1979). *Reading in the bilingual classroom: Literacy and biliteracy.* Retrieved December 21, 2005 from http://www.ncela.gwu.edu/pubs/classics/reading.

Halcón, J. (2001). Mainstream ideology and literacy instruction for Spanish-speaking children. In de la Luz-Reyes and Halcón (Eds.). *The best for our children: Critical perspectives on literacy for Latino students* (pp. 65–77). New York: Teachers College Press.

Hamayan, E.V. (1990). *Preparing mainstream classroom teachers to teach potentially English proficient students.* Proceedings of the 1st Research Symposium on Limited English Proficient Student Issues, Office of Bilingual Education & Minority Language Affairs. Retrieved September 11, 2003 from http://www.ncela.gwu.edu/ncbepubs/symposia/first/preparing.htm#top.

Jimenez, R. (2000). Literacy and the identity development of Latina/o students. *American Education Research Journal,* Volume 37, Number 4, pp. 971–1000.

John-Steiner, V. (1992). Private speech among adults. In R.M. Diaz & L.E. Berk (Eds.), *Private speech: From social interaction to self-regulation.* (pp. 285–296). Hillsdale, NJ: Lawrence Earlbaum Associates.

John-Steiner, V. (1995). Cognitive pluralism: A sociocultural approach. *Mind, Culture, & Activity,* Volume 2, Winter, pp. 2–11.

John-Steiner, V. (1999). Sociocultural and feminist theory: Mutuality and relevance. In Chaiklin, Hedegaard, and Jensen, U.J. (Eds.), *Activity theory and social practice: Cultural-historical approaches.* (Chapter 11). Aarhus: Aarhus University Press.

John-Steiner, V.P. (1991). Cognitive pluralism: A Whorfian analysis. In R.L. Cooper & B. Spolsky (Eds), *The influence of language on culture and thought* (pp. 61–74). Berlin: Mouton de Gryter.

John-Steiner, V., and Mahn, H. (1996). Sociohistorical approaches to learning and development: A Vygotskian framework. *Educational Psychologist,* Volume 31, (3/4), pp. 191–206.

John-Steiner, V., Meehan, T.M., and Mahn, H. (1998). A functional systems approach to concept development. *Mind, Culture, & Activity,* Volume 5, Number 2, 127–134.

John-Steiner, V., and Osterreich, H. (1975). Learning styles among Pueblo children. NIE Research Grant, Final Report, Albuquerque: University of New Mexico, Department of Educational Foundations.

John-Steiner, V., Panofsky, C., and Smith, L. (Eds.) (1994). *Sociocultural approaches to language & literacy: An interactionist perspective.* Cambridge: Cambridge University Press.

John-Steiner, V., and Souberman, E. (1978). Afterward. In L.S. Vygotsky, *Mind in society: The development of higher psychological processes.* (pp. 121–133). Cambridge, MA: Harvard University Press.

Kemmis, S., and McTaggart, R. (2000). Participatory action research. In Denzin and Lincoln, (Eds.) *Handbook of qualitative research*. (pp. 567–606). Thousand Oaks, CA: Sage Publications.

Kloss, H. (1977, 1998). *The American bilingual tradition*. Washington, DC: Center for Applied Linguistics.

Krashen, S.D. (1981). Bilingual education and second language acquisition theory. In *Schooling and language minority students: A theoretical framework*. (pp. 51–79). California State Department of Education.

LeCompte, M. D., and Preissle, J. (1993). *Ethnography and qualitative design in educational research*. (2nd ed.). San Diego, CA: Academic Press.

Lee, C.D., and Smagorinsky, P. (2000) (Eds.). *Vygotskian perspectives on literacy research: Constructing meaning through collaborative inquiry*. Cambridge: Cambridge University Press.

Lessow-Hurley, J. (2009). *The foundations of dual-language instruction*. (5th ed.) Boston, MA: Allyn and Bacon.

Lindholm-Leary, K., and Borsato, G. (2006). Academic achievement. In Genessee, et al., *Educating English language learners: A synthesis of research evidence* (pp. 176–211). New York: Cambridge University Press.

Mahn, H. (1997). *Dialogue journals: Perspectives of second language learners in a Vygotskian framework*. Doctoral dissertation: University of New Mexico.

Mahn, H., and John-Steiner, V. (2002). The gift of confidence: A Vygotskian view of emotions. In Wells and Claxon, (Eds.) *Learning for life in the 21rst century* (pp. 46–58). Oxford: Blackwell Publishers.

Moll, L.C. (Ed.) (1990). *Vygotsky and education: Instructional implications and applications of sociohistorical psychology*. Cambridge: Cambridge University Press.

Moll, L.C. (2001). The diversity of schooling: A cultural-historical approach. In de la Luz-Reyes and Halcón (Eds.). *The best for our children: Critical perspectives on literacy for Latino students* (pp. 13–28). New York: Teachers College Press.

National Center for Educational Statistics (NCES) (2003). *Status and trends in the education of Hispanics*. Retrieved September 9, 2003 from http://www.nces.ed.gov.pubs2003/hispanics.

National Center for Educational Statistics (NCES) (2010). *The Condition of education 2010*. Retrieved August 1, 2010 from http://www.nces.ed.gov/fastfacts/display/asp?id=96.

National Center for Educational Statistics (NCES) (2010). *The Condition of education 2010*. Retrieved August 1, 2010 from http://www.nces.ed.gov/pubs2010/2010015/indicator2_7.asp#1.

National Center for Educational Statistics (NCES) (2010). *The Condition of education 2010*. Retrieved:August 1, 2010 from http://www.nces.ed.gov/pubs2010/2010015/ tables/ table_7_1a.asp

Panofsky, C. (1999). *Getting to the heart of the matter: Literacy as value commitments*. Retrieved March 1, 2003, from http://www.fd.appstate.edu/arfonline/99_arfyearbook/pdf/ 2_panofsky_99.pdf

Pérez, B., and Torres-Guzmán, M.E. (1996). *Learning in two worlds: An integrated Spanish/English biliteracy approach*. (2nd Ed.) New York: Longman.

Pew Foundation, (2008). *Report on Hispanic students*. Retrieved August 1, 2010 from http://pewhispanic.org/files.reports/92.pdf.

Pew Foundation, (2006). *Report on Hispanic students*. Retrieved August 1, 2010 from http://pewhispanic.org/files.reports/72.pdf.

Reese, L., Garnier, H., Gallimore, R., and Goldenberg, C. (2000). Longitudinal analysis of the antecedents of emergent Spanish literacy and middle school English reading achievement of Spanish-speaking students. *American Educational Research Journal*, Volume 37, Number 3, pp. 633–662.

Riches, C., and Genesee, F. (2006). Chapter 3: Literacy: Cross-linguistic and cross-modal issues. In Genesee, et al., *Educating English language learners: A synthesis of research evidence* (pp. 64-87). New York: Cambridge University Press.

Royer, J., and Carlo, M. (1991). Transfer of comprehension skills from native to second language. *Journal of Reading*, 34 (6), pp. 450–455.

Siegler, R.S., and Crowley, K. (1991). The microgenetic method: A direct means for studying cognitive development. *American Psychologist*, Volume 46, pp. 606-620.

Stringer, E.T. (1999). *Action research: a handbook for practitioners*. (2nd ed.) Thousand Oaks, CA: Sage Publications.

Stringer, E.T. (2004). *Action research in education*. Upper Saddle River, NJ: Prentice-Hall.

Thomas, W.P., and Collier, V., (1997). *School effectiveness for language minority students*. NCBE Resource Collection Series #9, December.

Thomas, W.P., and Collier, V. (2002). *A national study of school effectiveness for language minority students' long-term academic achievement: Final report*. Center for Research in Education, Diversity, & Excellence. Retrieved November 23, 2005 from www.crede.org/research/llaa/1.1final.html

United States Census, Population Information (2000). Retrieved February 24, 2005 from www.census.gov/population/www.index.html.

Vygotsky, L.S. (1962). *Thought and language*. Cambridge, MA: The MIT Press. Published originally in Russian in 1934. Retrieved February 24, 2004 from http://www.marxists.org/archive/vygotsky/works/words.

Vygotsky, L.S. (1978). *Mind in society: The development of higher psychological processes*. London: Harvard University Press.

Vygotsky, L.S. (1981). The genesis of higher mental functions. In J.V. Wertsch (Ed.) *The concept of activity in Soviet psychology*. (pp. 144–188). Armonk, NY: Sharpe.

Vygotsky, L. (1986). *Thought and language*. Cambridge, MA: MIT Press.

Vygotsky, L. S. (1987a). *Thinking and speaking: The problem and the approach*. Retrieved April 29, 2003 from www.marxists.org/archive/vygotsky/works/words/lev1.htm.

Vygotsky, L.S. (1987b). *Thinking and speech: Written, inner, and oral speech*. Retrieved April 29, 2003 from www.marxists.org/archive/vygotsky/works/words/lev1.htm.

Vygotsky, L. S. (1994). In Van Der Veer, and Valsiner, *The Vygotsky reader*. Cambridge, MA: Blackwell Publishers.

Vygotsky, L.S. (1997a). The pre-history of the development of written language. In R. W. Rieber (Ed.) *The collected works of L.S. Vygotsky. Volume IV: The history of the development of higher mental functions* (pp.131–148). New York: Plenum Press.

Vygotsky, L.S. (1997b). The question of multilingual children. In R.W. Rieber (Ed.) *The collected works of L.S. Vygotsky. Volume IV: The history of the development of higher mental functions.* (pp. 253–259). New York: Plenum Press.

Wells, G., and Claxton, G. (Eds.). (2002). *Learning for life in the 21rst century*. Oxford: Blackwell Publishers.

Wertsch, J. (1985). Vygotsky's genetic method. In Wertsch. *Vygotsky and the social formation of mind*. (pp. 17–57). Cambridge, MA: Harvard University Press.

Index

Educational PSYCHOLOGY

Critical Pedagogical Perspectives

Greg S. Goodman, *General Editor*

Educational Psychology: Critical Pedagogical Perspectives is a series of relevant and dynamic works by scholars and practitioners of critical pedagogy, critical constructivism, and educational psychology. Reflecting a multitude of social, political, and intellectual developments prompted by the mentor Paulo Freire, books in the series enliven the educator's process with theory and practice that promote personal agency, social justice, and academic achievement. Often countering the dominant discourse with provocative and yet practical alternatives, *Educational Psychology: Critical Pedagogical Perspectives* speaks to educators on the forefront of social change and those who champion social justice.

For further information about the series and submitting manuscripts, please contact:

> Dr. Greg S. Goodman
> Department of Education
> Clarion University
> Clarion, Pennsylvania
> *ggoodman@clarion.edu*

To order other books in this series, please contact our Customer Service Department at:

> (800) 770-LANG (within the U.S.)
> (212) 647-7706 (outside the U.S.)
> (212) 647-7707 FAX

Or browse online by series at:

> www.peterlang.com